my revision notes

AS Edexcel History
RUSSIA IN REVOLUTION
1881–1924

Mark Gosling

Series editors:
Robin Bunce and
Laura Gallagher

HODDER
EDUCATION
AN HACHETTE UK COMPANY

Every effort has been made to trace all copyright holders, but if any have been inadvertently overlooked the Publishers will be pleased to make the necessary arrangements at the first opportunity.

Although every effort has been made to ensure that website addresses are correct at time of going to press, Hodder Education cannot be held responsible for the content of any website mentioned in this book. It is sometimes possible to find a relocated web page by typing in the address of the home page for a website in the URL window of your browser.

Hachette UK's policy is to use papers that are natural, renewable and recyclable products and made from wood grown in sustainable forests. The logging and manufacturing processes are expected to conform to the environmental regulations of the country of origin.

Orders: please contact Bookpoint Ltd, 130 Milton Park, Abingdon, Oxon OX14 4SB. Telephone: +44 (0)1235 827720. Fax: +44 (0)1235 400454. Lines are open 9.00a.m.–5.00p.m., Monday to Saturday, with a 24-hour message answering service. Visit our website at www.hoddereducation.co.uk.

© Mark Gosling 2011
First published in 2011 by
Hodder Education,
an Hachette UK company
338 Euston Road
London NW1 3BH

Impression number   5 4 3
Year   2016 2015 2014 2013

All rights reserved. Apart from any use permitted under UK copyright law, no part of this publication may be reproduced or transmitted in any form or by any means, electronic or mechanical, including photocopying and recording, or held within any information storage and retrieval system, without permission in writing from the publisher or under licence from the Copyright Licensing Agency Limited. Further details of such licences (for reprographic reproduction) may be obtained from the Copyright Licensing Agency Limited, Saffron House, 6–10 Kirby Street, London EC1N 8TS.

Typeset in Stempel Schneidler Light 11pt by Pantek Media, Maidstone, Kent
Artwork by Pantek Media
Printed and bound in India

A catalogue record for this title is available from the British Library

ISBN 978 1 444 15210 4

Contents

Introduction — 2

Revised **Section 1: The challenges to the Tsarist state, 1881–1906** — 4

- The extent of change in Russia, 1881–1894 — 4
- The impact of Witte's policies on Russia, 1892–1903 — 6
- The nature of Nicholas II's regime and the effectiveness of his rule — 8
- Political opposition to the Tsarist system of rule — 10
- The causes of the 1905 Russian Revolution — 12
- Key events and consequences of the 1905 Revolution — 14
- Exam focus — 16

Revised **Section 2: Tsarism's last chance, 1906–1917** — 18

- The role and impact of the Dumas, 1906–1914 — 18
- Why was Stolypin important in the period 1906–1911? — 20
- The impact of the First World War on the Russian armed forces — 22
- The impact of the First World War on Russian politics and economy — 24
- Causes of the Russian Revolution, February 1917 — 26
- The February Revolution — 28
- Exam focus — 30

Revised **Section 3: February to October 1917** — 32

- Difficulties facing the Provisional Government — 32
- The impact of Lenin's return to Russia in April 1917 — 34
- The significance of the July Days and General Kornilov — 36
- The key events of the October 1917 Revolution — 38
- The extent of Bolshevik support in October 1917 — 40
- Why did the Bolsheviks succeed in October 1917? — 42
- Exam focus — 44

Revised **Section 4: Keeping and consolidating power, 1918–1924** — 46

- Establishment of the Sovnarkom and closing of the Constituent Assembly — 46
- Early measures to secure Communist control and establishment of the Police State — 48
- The causes of the Russian Civil War — 50
- Reasons for the Communist victory and the importance of War Communism — 52
- The causes and impact of New Economic Policy (NEP) — 54
- The establishment of the USSR in 1922 and the death of Lenin — 56
- Exam focus — 58
- Timeline — 60
- Glossary — 62
- Answers — 65

Introduction

About Unit 1

Unit 1 is worth 50 per cent of your AS level. It requires detailed knowledge of a historical period and the ability to explain the causes, consequences and significance of historical events. There are no sources in the Unit 1 exam and therefore all marks available are awarded for use of your own knowledge.

In the exam, you are required to answer two questions from a range of options. The exam lasts for one hour and twenty minutes, unless you have been awarded extra time. The questions are all worth 30 marks and therefore you should divide your time equally between the questions.

The questions you answer must be on different topics. This book deals exclusively with Topic D3: Russia in Revolution 1881–1924: From Autocracy to Dictatorship. However, you must also be prepared to answer a question on another topic.

The exam will test your ability to:

- select information that focuses on the question
- organise this information to provide an answer to the question
- show range and depth in the examples you provide
- analyse the significance of the information used to reach an overall judgement.

Russia in Revolution, 1881–1924: From Autocracy to Dictatorship

The exam board specifies that students should study four general areas as part of this topic:

1. The challenges to the Tsarist state, 1881–1906.
2. Tsarism's last chance, 1906–1917: the Dumas; Stolypin; the impact of war; the downfall of the Romanovs.
3. February to October 1917: the Provisional Government and the Bolshevik coup.
4. Holding on to and consolidating power, 1918–1924: the civil war; changing economic policies; creating the Soviet state.

How to use this book

This book has been designed to help you to develop the knowledge and skills necessary to succeed in the exam. The book is divided into four sections – one for each general area of the course. Each section is made up of a series of topics organised into double-page spreads. On the left-hand page, you will find a summary of the key content you need to learn. Words in bold in the key content are defined in the glossary (pages 62–64). On the right-hand page, you will find exam-focused activities. Together, these two strands of the book will take you through the knowledge and skills essential for exam success.

▼ Key historical content ▼ Exam-focused activities

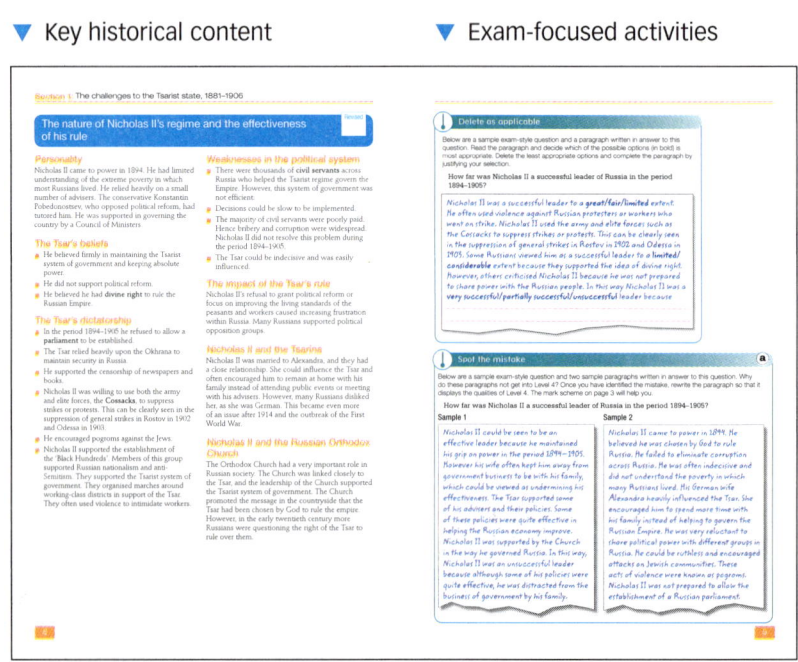

There are three levels of exam-focused activities:

- Band 1 activities are designed to develop the foundational skills needed to pass the exam. These have a turquoise heading and this symbol:
- Band 2 activities are designed to build on the skills developed in Band 1 activities and to help you achieve a C grade. These have an orange heading and this symbol:
- Band 3 activities are designed to enable you to access the highest grades. These have a purple heading and this symbol:

Some of the activities have answers or suggested answers on pages 65–70 and have the following symbol to indicate this: (a)

Others are intended for you to complete in pairs and assess by comparing answers and these don't have answers given at the back of the book.

Each section ends with an exam-style question and model A grade answer with examiner's commentary. This should give you guidance on what is required to achieve the top grades.

You can also keep track of your revision by ticking off each topic heading in the book, or by ticking the checklist on the contents page. Tick each box when you have:

- revised and understood a topic
- completed the activities.

Mark scheme

For some of the activities in the book it will be useful to refer to the mark scheme for the unit. Below is the mark scheme for Unit 1.

Level	Marks	Description
1	1–6	• Lacks focus on the question. • Limited factual accuracy. • Highly generalised. *Level 1 answers are highly simplistic, irrelevant or vague.*
2	7–12	• General points with some focus on the question. • Some accurate and relevant supporting evidence. *Level 2 answers might tell the story without addressing the question, or address the question without providing supporting examples.*
3	13–18	• General points that focus on the question. • Accurate support, but this may be either only partly relevant or lacking detail, or both. • Attempted analysis. *Level 3 answers attempt to focus on the question, but have significant areas of weakness. For example, the focus on the question may drift, the answer may lack specific examples, or parts of the essay may simply tell the story. Answers that do not deal with factors that are stated in the question cannot achieve higher than Level 3.*
4	19–24	• General points that clearly focus on the question and show understanding of the most important factors involved. • Accurate, relevant and detailed supporting evidence. • Analysis. *Level 4 answers clearly attempt to answer the question and demonstrate a detailed and wide-ranging knowledge of the period studied.*
5	25–30	• As Level 4. • Sustained analysis. *Level 5 answers are thorough and detailed. They clearly engage with the question and offer a balanced and carefully reasoned argument, which is sustained throughout the essay.*

3

Section 1:
The challenges to the Tsarist state, 1881–1906

The extent of change in Russia, 1881–1894

Alexander III and his policies

Alexander II, Tsar of Russia from 1855 to 1881, introduced important **reforms**, such as the emancipation of the **serfs** in 1861. Following Alexander II's assassination in 1881, the new Tsar, Alexander III, halted many of his reforms. The **conservative** Konstantin Pobedonostsev, known for the slogan '**Autocracy**, **Orthodoxy** and **Nationality**', influenced Alexander III. As **Chief Procurator of the Holy Synod**, Alexander III was very powerful. He linked the assassination directly to Alexander II's reforms and argued that they encouraged **radicalism**, which threatened the existence of the Tsarist system. Alexander III launched a campaign of **repression**, and in 1881 thousands of people were arrested.

Alexander III used the following measures to secure his power:

- Reforming ministers such as Loris-Melikov were forced to resign.
- A **manifesto** was introduced that emphasised the absolute political power of the Tsar.
- The 'Statute of State Security' law was passed, and established government-controlled courts. Suspects could be put on trial without a jury.
- Press freedoms were restricted. Fourteen major newspapers were banned between 1882 and 1889.
- Foreign books and newspapers were censored.
- The **Okhrana** became powerful and feared.
- University fees were increased and only the wealthy could attend.

Failed assassination of Alexander III, 1887

Repression increased after a failed assassination attempt on Alexander III in 1887. In 1889 '**Land Captains**' from the landed classes were introduced to help rule Russia. They were appointed directly by the Minister of Interior. In 1890 they became members of the **Zemstva**. Only the landed classes could vote people onto the Zemstva. Central government control was also extended over education. It was nearly impossible for the children of peasants and workers to gain an education beyond primary school. The government extended their influence over the judicial system, and, after 1890, had the right to choose juries in court cases.

Extending power over the Empire

Alexander III strengthened **Russification** within the Empire. In 1885, Russian became the official language of the Empire and all other languages were banned in schools. Jews were heavily persecuted within the Empire and experienced vicious **pogroms**.

Economic modernisation of Russia

Alexander III knew that Russia needed a modern economy to compete with international rivals such as Britain. Nikolai Bunge became Alexander's Finance Minister in 1881 and in 1882 he reduced the amount of tax paid by peasants. He established a Peasant Land Bank to provide financial support to the peasants, which would allow them to increase the size of their farms and agricultural production.

In 1887 Ivan Vyshnegradsky became Finance Minister. He introduced incentives for peasants to move to Siberia, where cheaper land was available, and encouraged foreign countries to loan Russia money for economic modernisation. However, such reforms did not prevent Russia experiencing a severe famine during 1891–1892, when between 1.5 and 2 million people died.

Spectrum of significance

Below are a sample exam-style question and a list of general points which could be used to answer the question. Use your own knowledge and the information on the opposite page to reach a judgement about the importance of these general points to the question posed. Write numbers on the spectrum below to indicate their relative importance. Having done this, write a brief justification of your placement, explaining why some of these factors are more important than others. The resulting diagram could form the basis of an essay plan.

How far did Alexander III reform Russia in the period 1881–94?

1. Higher education opportunities.
2. Government interfered with the courts.
3. Pogroms against the Jews became more common.
4. Russification was strengthened.
5. Economic reforms were introduced to modernise Russia.

⟵──────────────────────────⟶

Very important changes   Less important changes

Delete as applicable

Below are a sample exam-style question and a paragraph written in answer to this question. Read the paragraph and decide which of the possible options (in bold) is most appropriate. Delete the least appropriate options and complete the paragraph by justifying your selection.

How accurate is it to say that Alexander III made no significant changes in Russia in the period 1881–94?

> The extent of Alexander III's reforms were **limited/considerable** in the period 1881–1894. Nikolai Bunge, Alexander's finance minister in 1882, reduced the amount of tax paid by peasants. He established a Peasant Land Bank to provide financial support to the peasants, which would allow them to increase the size of their farms and agricultural production. However, other key reforms he introduced focused on extending the power of his own government. Arguably this meant that the extent of change in Russia was **significant/limited** during the rule of Alexander III. The famine of 1891–1892 supports the argument that Alexander III **failed/succeeded** in changing Russia to a **great/limited** degree in this period.

Section 1: The challenges to the Tsarist state, 1881–1906

The impact of Witte's policies on Russia, 1892–1903

Revised

Russian economy and society

The emancipation of the serfs in 1861 did not resolve the problems of agricultural production by the end of the nineteenth century. This was very evident with the famine of 1891–1892. Some developments to improve the Russian economy occurred in the 1880s. The introduction of **tariffs** to encourage the domestic buying of Russian goods was implemented in 1891. However, Russia was still behind Western Europe in terms of economic development.

Impact of Sergei Witte and the 'Great Spurt', 1892–1903

The key goal of Sergei Witte, the Minister of Finance, was to strengthen Russia economically and maintain Russia's position as a Great Power. Witte knew that Russia suffered from the following problems in the late nineteenth century:

- More foreign investment was needed to develop Russia's economy.
- Russia needed a larger business class.
- Russia needed more peasants to move to the cities to work in the factories.

Witte implemented the following policies to modernise the Russian economy:

- Government became more active in developing the economy.
- Greater emphasis was placed on producing more coal, iron and steel.
- Loans were obtained from countries such as France.
- Taxes on peasants were increased to fund industrialisation.
- The **Trans-Siberian Railway** was built to exploit Siberia economically.
- In 1897 Witte introduced laws to restrict working hours to 11.5 a day for all workers.

The success and failures of Witte's policies

Successes

- Coal and iron production increased. In the 1890s industrial growth increased by 8 per cent per year.
- Between 1897 and 1900 Russia received 144 million roubles in foreign investment.
- By 1903 the Trans-Siberian Railway was almost completed. Railway building across Russia was expanded.
- Large factories emerged in important cities such as St Petersburg and Moscow.
- Cities grew rapidly. St Petersburg's population grew from 1 million in 1890 to approximately 2 million in 1914.
- Resources in Siberia were increasingly exploited.
- Economic modernisation allowed Russia to equip their armed forces with more sophisticated weaponry and compete as a world Great Power.

Failures

- Living conditions in the cities for the working classes were very poor.
- More political opposition emerged against the Tsarist system of government.
- Strikes became more common in Russian cities.
- Increased taxes on the peasants caused widespread anger.
- Witte's reforms did not result in Russia overtaking countries such as Germany economically.
- By 1913 industry contributed only 20 per cent of national income and only 18 per cent of Russians lived in towns.
- Russia was in more debt than any other European country. In 1914 Russia owed 8 billion roubles.
- The Russian political system did not modernise and educational opportunities remained limited for the majority.
- Russia was modernising from a position that was further behind the economies of other countries.

Complete the paragraph

Below are a sample exam-style question and a paragraph written in answer to this question. The paragraph contains a point and specific examples, but lacks a concluding explanatory link back to the question. Complete the paragraph adding this link in the space provided.

How far do you agree that Sergei Witte's policies were successful in modernising the Russian economy in the period 1892–1904?

> Sergei Witte's policies were successful in modernising Russia's economy by 1903 to a considerable extent. Witte wanted Russia to become a world power through industrialisation. He obtained loans from France in order to build the Trans-Siberian Railway. The railway was designed to promote better links across Russia and to stimulate industry. He raised taxes from the peasants to help support industrialisation, and between 1892 and 1903 there was considerable urbanisation as people moved from the countryside to get jobs in the cities.

 Support or challenge?

Below is a sample exam-style question, which asks how far you agree with a specific statement. Below this is a series of general statements that are relevant to the question. Using your own knowledge and the information on the opposite page, decide whether these statements support or challenge the statement in the question and tick the appropriate box.

'Sergei Witte's attempts to modernise the Russian economy were very successful in the period 1892–1904.' How far do you agree with this judgement?

	SUPPORT	CHALLENGE
Russia received 144 million roubles in foreign investment between 1897 and 1900.		
In 1914 Russia owed 8 billion roubles.		
By 1903 the Trans-Siberian Railway was almost completed.		
By 1913 industry contributed only 20 per cent of national income and only 18 per cent of Russians lived in towns.		
St Petersburg's population grew from 1 million in 1890 to approximately 2 million in 1914.		
In 1897 Witte passed laws which restricted working hours to 11.5 a day for all Russian workers.		
In the 1890s industrial growth increased by 8 per cent per year.		
Economic modernisation allowed Russia to equip its armed forces with more sophisticated weaponry.		

Section 1: The challenges to the Tsarist state, 1881–1906

The nature of Nicholas II's regime and the effectiveness of his rule

Personality

Nicholas II came to power in 1894. He had limited understanding of the extreme poverty in which most Russians lived. He relied heavily on a small number of advisers. The conservative Konstantin Pobedonostsev, who opposed political reform, had tutored him. He was supported in governing the country by a Council of Ministers.

The Tsar's beliefs

- He believed firmly in maintaining the Tsarist system of government and keeping absolute power.
- He did not support political reform.
- He believed he had **divine right** to rule the Russian Empire.

The Tsar's dictatorship

- In the period 1894–1905 he refused to allow a **parliament** to be established.
- The Tsar relied heavily upon the Okhrana to maintain security in Russia.
- He supported the censorship of newspapers and books.
- Nicholas II was willing to use both the army and elite forces, the **Cossacks**, to suppress strikes or protests. This can be clearly seen in the suppression of general strikes in Rostov in 1902 and Odessa in 1903.
- He encouraged pogroms against the Jews.
- Nicholas II supported the establishment of the 'Black Hundreds'. Members of this group supported Russian nationalism and anti-Semitism. They supported the Tsarist system of government. They organised marches around working-class districts in support of the Tsar. They often used violence to intimidate workers.

Weaknesses in the political system

- There were thousands of **civil servants** across Russia who helped the Tsarist regime govern the Empire. However, this system of government was not efficient:
- Decisions could be slow to be implemented.
- The majority of civil servants were poorly paid. Hence bribery and corruption were widespread. Nicholas II did not resolve this problem during the period 1894–1905.
- The Tsar could be indecisive and was easily influenced.

The impact of the Tsar's rule

Nicholas II's refusal to grant political reform or focus on improving the living standards of the peasants and workers caused increasing frustration within Russia. Many Russians supported political opposition groups.

Nicholas II and the Tsarina

Nicholas II was married to Alexandra, and they had a close relationship. She could influence the Tsar and often encouraged him to remain at home with his family instead of attending public events or meeting with his advisers. However, many Russians disliked her, as she was German. This became even more of an issue after 1914 and the outbreak of the First World War.

Nicholas II and the Russian Orthodox Church

The Orthodox Church had a very important role in Russian society. The Church was linked closely to the Tsar, and the leadership of the Church supported the Tsarist system of government. The Church promoted the message in the countryside that the Tsar had been chosen by God to rule the empire. However, in the early twentieth century more Russians were questioning the right of the Tsar to rule over them.

Delete as applicable

Below are a sample exam-style question and a paragraph written in answer to this question. Read the paragraph and decide which of the possible options (in bold) is most appropriate. Delete the least appropriate options and complete the paragraph by justifying your selection.

How far was Nicholas II a successful leader of Russia in the period 1894–1905?

> Nicholas II was a successful leader to a **great/fair/limited** extent. He often used violence against Russian protesters or workers who went on strike. Nicholas II used the army and elite forces such as the Cossacks to suppress strikes or protests. This can be clearly seen in the suppression of general strikes in Rostov in 1902 and Odessa in 1903. Some Russians viewed him as a successful leader to a **limited/considerable** extent because they supported the idea of divine right. However, others criticised Nicholas II because he was not prepared to share power with the Russian people. In this way Nicholas II was a **very successful/partially successful/unsuccessful** leader because
> _____
> _____

Spot the mistake

Below are a sample exam-style question and two sample paragraphs written in answer to this question. Why do these paragraphs not get into Level 4? Once you have identified the mistake, rewrite the paragraph so that it displays the qualities of Level 4. The mark scheme on page 3 will help you.

How far was Nicholas II a successful leader of Russia in the period 1894–1905?

Sample 1

> Nicholas II could be seen to be an effective leader because he maintained his grip on power in the period 1894–1905. However his wife often kept him away from government business to be with his family, which could be viewed as undermining his effectiveness. The Tsar supported some of his advisers and their policies. Some of these policies were quite effective in helping the Russian economy improve. Nicholas II was supported by the Church in the way he governed Russia. In this way, Nicholas II was an unsuccessful leader because although some of his policies were quite effective, he was distracted from the business of government by his family.

Sample 2

> Nicholas II came to power in 1894. He believed he was chosen by God to rule Russia. He failed to eliminate corruption across Russia. He was often indecisive and did not understand the poverty in which many Russians lived. His German wife Alexandra heavily influenced the Tsar. She encouraged him to spend more time with his family instead of helping to govern the Russian Empire. He was very reluctant to share political power with different groups in Russia. He could be ruthless and encouraged attacks on Jewish communities. These acts of violence were known as pogroms. Nicholas II was not prepared to allow the establishment of a Russian parliament.

9

Section 1: The challenges to the Tsarist state, 1881–1906

Political opposition to the Tsarist system of rule

Revised

Reasons for opposition

There was a long history of opposition to the Tsar's autocratic rule in the nineteenth century. Some opposition groups resorted to violent tactics. The **'People's Will'** assassinated Alexander II in 1881. Towards the end of the nineteenth century, more Russians wanted a complete change in the way Russia was ruled. A growing middle class began to demand **constitutional government** and political freedom. Many peasants and workers wanted higher living standards and an end to extreme poverty. Other groups supported the ideas of Karl Marx.

The impact of Marxism

Karl Marx argued that **capitalism** resulted in the exploitation of the workers, and that the workers would rise up against the ruling classes and remove capitalism. A **communist** society would emerge which would be fairer and there would be no class struggle. The accelerated industrialisation of Russia in the 1890s and early twentieth century increased the appeal of **Marxism** to working-class Russians and resulted in new political parties emerging.

Political opposition groups

The Social Democratic Party	The Socialist Revolutionaries	The Liberals
<ul><li>The Russian Social Democratic Party was a Marxist party established in 1898.</li><li>The Social Democrats failed to agree on party organisation and strategy.</li><li>In 1903 the party split into two groups: the **Bolsheviks**, 'men of the majority' and the **Mensheviks**, 'men of the minority'.</li><li>The Bolsheviks, led by **Lenin**, believed that a revolution could only be brought about by a small, secretive, elite group of dedicated Communist revolutionaries.</li><li>The Mensheviks believed that a revolution should be carried out by a mass party which was open to the whole working class.</li></ul>	<ul><li>The **Socialist Revolutionaries** drew on some of the ideas of Marxism and were led by **Victor Chernov**.</li><li>They focused on attracting the support of the peasants.</li><li>Peasants experienced economic difficulties in the early twentieth century, which made the Socialist Revolutionaries more popular.</li><li>The Socialist Revolutionaries had no coherent long-term plan to achieve power and were often poorly organised.</li><li>One of their key methods was terrorism. They were responsible for the assassination of **Plehve** the Minister of Interior in 1904.</li></ul>	<ul><li>Industrialisation had resulted in a growing educated middle class.</li><li>Many supported liberalism and wanted to adopt a modern western European style of democratic government, and rejected the ideas of Marxism.</li><li>There were demands for a new political constitution, which was rejected by Nicholas II before 1905.</li><li>In the early twentieth century, liberal politicians became more aggressive in their demands. **Pavel Miliukov** and **Pyotr Struve** demanded political reforms such as free elections and freedom of speech and the press.</li><li>In 1904, Struve organised public protests to demand more concessions from the Tsar.</li><li>After the 1905 Revolution, two main **Liberal** groups emerged known as the **Kadets** and **Octobrists**. The Kadets wanted further political reforms after 1905, whilst the Octobrists fully accepted the reforms proposed in the October Manifesto. The Octobrists did not campaign for further significant changes to the Russian Constitution after 1905.</li></ul>

Develop the detail

Below are a sample exam-style question and a paragraph written in answer to this question. The paragraph contains a limited amount of detail. Annotate the paragraph to add additional detail to the answer.

> How far was political opposition to the Tsar divided in their aims and methods in the period 1881–1905?

There were many different political groups that opposed the Tsarist system of government and they were divided to a considerable extent. The Social Democrats were a single united party when they were established in 1898. However, the party split between two different groups and they had different beliefs and aims. The Socialist Revolutionaries also emerged as an opposition group and had support from many Russians. They were also prepared to use violence like some other groups to achieve their aims. The Liberals wanted political reforms but the Tsar refused to meet most of their demands. Therefore to a great degree political parties were divided amongst themselves and with each other in the period 1881–1905.

Turning assertion into argument

Below are a sample exam-style question and a series of assertions. Read the question and then add a justification to each of the assertions to turn it into an argument.

> How far were the political opponents of the Tsar divided in their aims and methods in the period 1881–1905?

The Social Democratic Party became very divided in the sense that

The Socialist Revolutionaries and the Liberals had different aims and methods in the sense that

Revolutionary ideas appealed to many Russians in the sense that

Section 1: The challenges to the Tsarist state, 1881–1906

The causes of the 1905 Russian Revolution

Key background factors

The process of industrialisation begun by Witte in the 1890s encouraged more people to move to the cities. The population of Russia expanded rapidly from 98 million in 1885 to 125 million by 1905. However, in the early twentieth century there was an economic slowdown and fewer jobs became available. Large **slums** developed in cities such as St Petersburg. This resulted in workers becoming more rebellious in the period 1901–1905. Poor agricultural techniques and poor government resulted in a crisis in agriculture, with famines occurring in 1901.

The government was also experiencing more political challenges from terrorists. In 1905 the Grand Duke Sergei, the Tsar's uncle, was assassinated by a member of the Socialist Revolutionaries. The educated middle classes were also demanding more political reforms. Finally a disastrous war with Japan in 1905 triggered protests and rebellions within Russia.

1904: Government concessions

In 1904 it appeared that the government was more prepared to listen to the demands of the Liberals, and this raised expectations for political reform. In April 1904 the conservative Minister of Interior was replaced by the more liberal Svyatopolk-Mirsky. He supported a more liberal approach and granted more press freedoms. This appointment encouraged Pyotr Struve to set up the 'Union of Liberation', which sought more political freedoms. However, in 1904 the Tsar largely ignored these demands.

Key trigger causes

The Russo-Japanese War of 1905 and its impact	The Bloody Sunday protest of January 1905 and its impact
• The Japanese inflicted humiliating defeats on the Russian army and navy in the Far East. • The Russians were forced to surrender Port Arthur in January 1905. • The Russian Baltic fleet sailed around the world to confront the Japanese navy and was defeated at the Battle of Tsushima in May 1905. • These defeats ignited rebellions and protests across Russia. • The Tsar was forced to sign a humiliating peace treaty with Japan. • The war also meant the Tsar had fewer troops within Russia to control protests in the cities.	• Workers in St Petersburg launched protests and produced a **petition**, demanding an eight-hour working day and an elected assembly. • A priest called Father Gapon led the protesters. They marched to the Winter Palace in January to present the petition to the Tsar. • The march numbered 150,000 people. • The local authorities had to rely on the army to maintain control. • The soldiers opened fire on the crowd and over 200 people were killed. • The massacre became known as 'Bloody Sunday' and helped to unite different groups. Protests became more frequent. • In February 1905, 400,000 workers went on strike as a consequence of the massacre. • There were **mutinies** by some of the armed forces, such as on the battleship *Potemkin*. The majority of the army remained loyal to the Tsar. • The government began to make concessions to avoid a revolution within Russia.

Simple essay style

Below is a sample exam-style question. Use your own knowledge and the information on the opposite page to produce a plan for this question. Choose four general points, and provide three pieces of specific information to support each general point. Once you have planned your essay, write the introduction and conclusion for the essay. The introduction should list the points to be discussed in the essay. The conclusion should summarise the key points and justify which point was the most important.

> How far was the Tsar's failure to share political power responsible for widespread rebellions and protests in 1905?

Eliminate irrelevance

Below are a sample exam-style question and a paragraph written in answer to this question. Read the paragraph and identify parts of the paragraph that are not directly relevant to the question. Draw a line through the information that is irrelevant and justify your deletions in the margin.

> How far was the Tsar's failure to share political power responsible for widespread rebellions and protests in 1905?

The Tsar's failure to share political power undoubtedly led to the unrest of 1905. Peasants and workers were becoming increasingly frustrated by the Tsar's failure to resolve poor agricultural policies, repeated famines and poor living standards within the cities. Because of the Tsar's failure to introduce political reform, many workers and peasants supported political opposition groups such as the Socialist Revolutionaries. One of the Tsar's leading advisers Sergei Witte helped to modernise the Russian economy by 1905. Nicholas II also failed to listen to the political demands of a growing Russian middle class, many of whom wanted Russia to become a parliamentary democracy, which to a degree made rebellion more likely. After 1905 the Tsar allowed the establishment of a Russian Parliament known as the Duma. The Tsar's failure to share real political power before 1905 did contribute to the protests and rebellions in 1905 to a substantial degree because he failed to give the peasants or workers any form of real political power.

13

Section 1: The challenges to the Tsarist state, 1881–1906

Key events and consequences of the 1905 Revolution

Key events

The disastrous defeats for the Russian army and navy in 1905 and the 'Bloody Sunday' massacre sparked widespread strikes and protests across Russia. By the end of 1905 over 2.7 million workers had been on strike, and a general strike developed between September and October of 1905. There were also peasant uprisings in areas such as Kursk. In July 1905 the first meeting of the All-Russian Peasants Union took place in Moscow. They demanded more political freedoms and the transfer of more land to the peasants from the nobility. In May 1905 Pavel Miliukov established the 'Union of Unions', which united leaders of the Zemstva and professional groups in demanding a new political constitution.

> ### The St Petersburg Soviet
> In St Petersburg, an assembly of workers was established known as the St Petersburg **Soviet**. This assembly represented 96 factories. The Mensheviks and Bolsheviks also participated in the Soviet, and it showed that the workers could organise themselves into an opposition group. The Soviet was closed down by Tsarist troops in December 1905.

December also saw an armed uprising in Moscow, resulting in over 1000 people being killed. The Bolsheviks played a key role in this revolt, which was crushed by loyal Tsarist soldiers. There were also mutinies in the Russian Baltic and Pacific navies in October 1905.

Consequences and the Tsar's response

In October 1905, Witte successfully persuaded the Tsar's government to issue the October Manifesto, which promised various political reforms. Significantly, it accepted the establishment of a **Duma**. It also acknowledged that there should be more political freedoms such as freedom of speech, assembly and press. Russian liberals welcomed these proposals and accepted it as a final piece of political reform. However, other liberals known as Kadets saw it as the beginning of political reform. The Socialist Revolutionaries, Mensheviks and Bolsheviks criticised the October Manifesto for being too limited and not meeting their own political aims.

After the October Manifesto, the Tsar was able to re-establish his authority. The armed forces largely remained loyal to the Tsar. The Tsar established a new political group called the 'Union of Russian People', which was linked to the 'Black Hundreds'. This group attacked and killed those who supported reform in the countryside and within the cities.

Weaknesses within the opposition

- Opposition groups were divided and often poorly organised, which made it easier for groups such as the 'Black Hundreds' to persecute and destroy them.
- Opposition leaders such as those of the St Petersburg Soviet were arrested in December 1905, which deprived the workers of their leadership.
- The Socialist Revolutionaries, Liberals, Mensheviks and Bolsheviks all had different political beliefs and aims.
- The October Manifesto was successful in further increasing these divisions.
- The Tsar had successfully secured his regime by 1906.

Develop the detail

Below are a sample exam-style question and a paragraph written in answer to this question. The paragraph contains a limited amount of detail. Annotate the paragraph to add additional detail to the answer.

How successful was the Tsar in addressing the problems he faced in 1905?

> The Tsar was largely successful in dealing with the problems he faced in 1905. Different political groups were very hostile to the Tsar, especially after humiliating defeats against the Japanese. However, he successfully divided these groups by promising political reforms. These different groups often failed to agree on their political aims, which made it easier for the Tsar to secure his regime by the end of 1905. Importantly the Tsar retained the support of the armed forces, although there were some mutinies in the navy. He also set up a new political party and some of his supporters killed some Russians who supported reform. Many opponents to the Tsar were arrested and the army crushed various protests ruthlessly. In this way, the Tsar was largely successful in addressing the problems he faced in 1905 because he crushed the revolution without conceding real reform.

Spectrum of significance

Below are a sample exam-style question and a list of general points which could be used to answer the question. Use your own knowledge and the information on the opposite page to reach a judgement about the importance of these general points to the question posed. Write numbers on the spectrum below to indicate their relative importance. Having done this, write a brief justification of your placement, explaining why some of these factors are more important than others. The resulting diagram could form the basis of an essay plan.

How successful was the Tsar in addressing the problems he faced in 1905?

1. Divisions amongst the Tsar's political opponents.
2. The loyalty of the Russian army.
3. The October Manifesto.
4. The role of the Black Hundreds.
5. Arrests of different leaders.
6. The role of Witte.

⟵────────────────────────────⟶

Very successful   Not very successful

Section 1: The challenges to the Tsarist state, 1881–1906

Exam focus

Below is a sample A grade essay. Read it and the examiner comments around it.

> Why did widespread protests and rebellions occur across Russia in 1905?

The introduction is focused and begins to directly answer the question. The candidate also indicates some important issues, which they later discuss in the main body of the essay.

Many different factors contributed to the protests and rebellions in 1905. These range from the role of different political opposition groups such as the Bolsheviks and the failure of the Tsar to pass political reforms. The Russo-Japanese war of 1905 acted as the trigger to the rebellions. However, many factors such as increasing social discontent within the cities and countryside were also important and these issues can be linked back to key developments in the late nineteenth century.

The candidate effectively links the impact of Witte's economic policies to growing discontent in the cities and countryside.

Witte's economic reforms of the 1890s and early 1900s contributed to the rebellions of 1905. Accelerated industrialisation resulted in the dramatic growth of Russian cities. The population of Russia also grew dramatically in this period from 98 million in 1885 to 125 million by 1905. This placed more pressure on the land and within the cities. More peasants wanted land to be redistributed from the corrupt nobility. These demands grew after famines in the 1890s and in 1901. The number of workers in the cities grew, resulting in large slums. The living standards within these slums were very poor and in the early twentieth century the Russian economy began to slow down. Wages did not rise dramatically and poverty increased. Witte's reforms contributed to the rebellions and protests of 1905, because the economic reform created unrest amongst the Tsar's subjects.

The candidate explores the role of political opposition groups and uses very precise examples to support their arguments.

The role of political opposition groups also needs to be considered when considering why protests developed in 1905. The Socialist Revolutionaries wanted the removal of the Tsar and redistribution of land to the peasants. These policies were widely supported by peasants. The Socialist Revolutionaries used violence and were responsible for the assassination of the Tsar's uncle, Grand Duke Sergei, in 1905. The Bolsheviks and Mensheviks also played a role by participating in the Petrograd Soviet in 1905. The Bolsheviks also helped organise and participated in the armed uprising in Moscow in December 1905. Liberals such as Pavel Miliuko, established political groups such as the 'Union of Unions' in May 1905 to demand more political reforms. These different groups helped to spread ideas, which encouraged people to oppose the Tsar in 1905.

> However, the failure of the Tsar to respond to demands for political reform also contributed to the rebellions of 1905. In the period 1894–1905 the Tsar was more influenced by conservative advisers. The Tsar believed in divine right and was not prepared to share power. He viewed constitutional reform as weakening his own power and going against the wishes of God. Therefore he allowed no liberalisation of his regime, and the people had no way of legally expressing their discontent. The Tsar's failure to allow reform led to rebellion in 1905 because ordinary Russians were allowed no other way of seeking change.
>
> The most significant factor in causing widespread protests in 1905 was the Russo-Japanese War. The war clearly revealed the weaknesses of the Tsarist system of government. The humiliating surrender of Port Arthur and the naval defeat at Tsushima proved to many Russians that the political system had to change and they resorted to protests to achieve their aims. The massacre in St Petersburg on 9 January 1905 known as 'Bloody Sunday' further supported this view and protests and rebellions became more widespread throughout 1905. The war was important because it increased support for political opposition groups who actively attempted to bring in political change or remove the Tsar by force.
>
> Throughout 1905 the protests and rebellions were caused by a variety of factors. If the Tsar had been less autocratic and more willing to listen to advice from a wider group of people the rebellions and protests may have been avoided. However, the Russo-Japanese war clearly revealed the flaws in the Tsarist system of government. It also showed how heavily the Tsar relied on the army to keep power, and this did not bode well for the future of the Tsarist regime.

The candidate considers causal significance and links different issues to justify their arguments.

The candidate reaches a clear conclusion and communicates their points very effectively. The candidate obviously has a firm grasp and understanding of this topic.

28/30

This essay easily reaches the highest marks. The candidate's answer has an explicit and sustained analytical focus. They have developed their arguments with precise factual examples. Additionally they have explored a range of issues and linked different causes to explore their answer in more depth. The answer is well structured and points have been communicated clearly.

Reverse engineering

The best essays are based on careful plans. Read the essay and the examiner's comments and try to work out the general points of the plan used to write the essay. Once you have done this, note down the specific examples used to support each general point.

Section 2:
Tsarism's last chance, 1906–1917

The role and impact of the Dumas, 1906–1914

Key developments in 1906
Stability was gradually restored to Russia in 1906 by the appointment of the decisive Pavel Durnovo as Minister of Interior. **Liberals** did not want Russia to slide into anarchy, therefore they co-operated with the regime. In April 1906 the Tsar, with the help of Witte, secured a desperately needed loan from France of 850 million roubles. Witte had struggled under the pressure of events in 1905 and was replaced by Pyotr Stolypin. He frequently used the death penalty to restore order in the countryside. In this context the Fundamental Laws of 1906 were introduced.

Fundamental Laws
These laws became the new constitution of Russia. They created a national **parliament**, with a lower house known as the **Duma** being elected. The upper house, known as the 'Council of State', consisted of elected members and those appointed by the Tsar. Article 87 of the Fundamental Laws allowed the Tsar to rule by **decree** and ignore parliament. The new parliament and its limited powers did not fulfil the demands of the Tsar's political opponents.

Political influence of the Dumas
The first Duma was elected in April 1906 and many of its members wanted land reforms. The Tsar dissolved this parliament after 73 days because they were making too many radical demands, such as the release of political prisoners. A second Duma was elected in February 1907 and passed important land reform laws supported by Stolypin. However, it still contained people who demanded further political reforms and lasted only three months. The police claimed that members of the Duma were encouraging mutinies in the armed forces, and this provided the Tsar with a reason to dissolve this Duma in June.

The Tsar and Stolypin decided to hold further elections for a new Duma in November 1907. However, only the wealthiest 30 per cent of men could vote. Consequently, there were few reformers in the new parliament as the wealthy were not in favour of radical reform. This election resulted in a Duma that did not demand reforms and supported the Tsar. Further land reforms were passed by this Duma, but became known by many Russians as the 'Duma of Lords and Lackeys'. Stolypin was assassinated in 1911 and a new Duma was elected in June 1912, which continued to support the Tsar.

The impact of the Dumas
- The third and fourth Dumas lasted until 1914 and did not fully support reform.
- However, they did have some positive impacts on Russia, such as **Land Captains** being replaced by more effective Justices of the Peace.
- A plan to establish universal primary education was introduced.
- Some health and accident insurance programmes were developed to help workers.
- Some improvements to the Russian armed forces were implemented.
- The establishment and continued existence of the Dumas moved Russia closer towards becoming a full democracy, even though the power of the Tsar still dominated in this period.

Develop the detail

Below are a sample exam-style question and a paragraph written in answer to this question. The paragraph contains a limited amount of detail. Annotate the paragraph to add additional detail to the answer.

How successful were the Dumas in the period 1906–1914?

> The Dumas had some successes in the period 1906–1914. They did pass some reforms, which helped some Russians. On occasions the Dumas worked with the Tsar's government effectively. However, the extent of success should not be over-emphasised. There were tensions between the Duma and Tsar especially between 1906 and 1907. Many people could not vote in the elections to the Dumas as the vote was restricted to certain groups after 1907 and this weakened opposition groups within the Duma. In this way the Dumas were moderately successful because although they did pass some reforms, they were unable to democratise Russia.

Delete as applicable

Below are a sample exam-style question and a paragraph written in answer to this question. Read the paragraph and decide which of the possible options (in bold) is most appropriate. Delete the least appropriate options and complete the paragraph by justifying your selection.

How successful were the Dumas in the period 1906–1914?

> The Dumas were successful to a **great/fair/limited** extent. For example, the second Duma introduced some important land reforms with the support of Stolypin. The third and fourth Dumas implemented improvements to the Russia armed forces and introduced health and insurance programmes for Russian workers. The existence of the Dumas marked an end to the complete autocratic power of the Tsar within Russia and provided a possible step towards full democracy. However, many Russians were still excluded from voting in elections for the Duma especially after 1907. In this way the Dumas were **extremely/moderately/slightly** successful because

Section 2: Tsarism's last chance, 1906–1917

Why was Stolypin important in the period 1906–1911?

Stolypin's role

Stolypin was the Prime Minister of Russia between 1906 and 1911. He was assassinated in 1911. He opposed revolutionary groups such as the **Bolsheviks** and supported **agrarian reforms**. Stolypin understood that making more peasants small landowners would prevent them supporting groups who opposed the Tsar, such as the **Socialist Revolutionaries**. Additionally it would help modernise Russian agriculture and make it more productive. By the end of 1907 he had ensured that the Tsar's supporters dominated the Duma.

Land reform

In November 1906, Stolypin passed a law that made it easier for peasants to break away from communes. Peasants no longer needed the permission of the majority of the members of the commune, or **Mir**. Also in November 1906, the Peasant Land Bank was encouraged to give more loans to peasants. In 1910 a law was passed which dissolved all Mirs where no land redistribution had taken place after the emancipation of the **serfs** in 1861. The Mirs had continued to use primitive and inefficient farming techniques.

Stolypin also provided incentives and government loans for peasants to move to land that had not been exploited in Siberia. Stolypin hoped that increasing the number of peasant landowners who farmed more efficiently would mean that fewer Russian peasants would be needed to farm the land. They would then have to move to the cities to gain employment, which would help meet the increasing demand for workers in the cities.

Impact of Stolypin's reforms

- In 1905, 20 per cent of peasants owned land. By 1915 this had increased to 50 per cent.
- Agricultural production increased from 45.9 million tonnes in 1906 to 61.7 million tonnes in 1913.
- The outbreak of the First World War in 1914 prevented further improvements, which had been previously initiated by Stolypin before his assassination in 1911.
- During this same period, little was done to improve living conditions for workers in the cities. Industrial unrest continued with the Lena Goldfield massacre of 1912 in Siberia, when the Tsar's police killed strikers.
- In June 1914 a general strike was declared in Moscow but was stopped after Russia entered the First World War. These strikes revealed that Stolypin's policies had not resolved economic and social tensions after his assassination in 1911.

The successes and failures of Stolypin's reforms

Successes	Failures
<ul><li>Between 1906 and 1907, 15 per cent of peasants accepted new opportunities presented by Stolypin's reforms.</li><li>Between 1906 and 1914, 25 per cent of peasants had left the Mirs.</li><li>Some peasants who owned land became more loyal to the Tsar.</li><li>The third and fourth Dumas did not threaten the Tsar.</li><li>Lenin saw Stolypin's reforms as a threat to gaining the support of peasants in any future revolution.</li></ul>	<ul><li>The majority of peasants who accepted Stolypin's incentives were located in the more prosperous areas of Russia, such as Southern Russia and the Ukraine.</li><li>His land reforms had a limited impact in the cities.</li><li>Stolypin weakened the Dumas.</li></ul>

Turning assertion into argument

Below is a sample exam-style question and a series of assertions. Read the question and then add a justification to each of the assertions to turn it into an argument.

How accurate is it to say that Stolypin's policies had a limited impact on Russia in the period 1906–1914?

> Stolypin's policies did have some impact on Russian peasants and agriculture in the sense that
>
> Stolypin's policies had less impact in Russian cities in the sense that
>
> Stolypin's policies did not increase the influence of the Dumas in the sense that
>
> The Tsar's position in Russia was strengthened by Stolypin's policies in the sense that

Spectrum of significance

Below are a sample exam-style question and a list of general points, which could be used to answer the question. Use your own knowledge and the information on the opposite page to reach a judgement about the importance of these general points to the question posed. Write numbers on the spectrum below to indicate their relative importance. Having done this, write a brief justification of your placement, explaining why some of these factors are more important than others. The resulting diagram could form the basis of an essay plan.

How accurate is it to say that Stolypin's policies had a limited impact on Russia in the period 1906–1914?

1. The impact of his policies towards the peasants.
2. The impact Stolypin had on the Dumas in the period 1906–1911.
3. The impact of his policies on the Russian working classes.
4. The strengthening of the Tsar's position within Russia.
5. The impact of Stolypin's policies on the political opposition towards the Tsar in Russia.
6. The impact of his policies on modernising the Russian economy.

Substantial impact ←————————————————→ Limited impact

Section 2: Tsarism's last chance, 1906–1917

The impact of the First World War on the Russian armed forces

The Russian army, 1906–1914

After 1905 the army needed strengthening. In 1908 military reforms focused on improving the organisation of the armed forces and ensuring they were provided with appropriate equipment. The regimental structure of the army was changed and types of artillery used by the army were standardised. The Russians had to decide to choose an offensive or defensive military strategy on its western borders. The French wanted the Russians to adopt an offensive strategy to put more pressure on Germany. Increased tensions in the Balkans resulted in the Russians adopting the 'Grand Plan' in 1913, which was developed by the Minister of War Vladimir Sukhomlinov. The plan supported an offensive strategy as demanded by the French.

The Russian armed forces and the First World War

In a long war, Russia's economy struggled to maintain supplies and equipment to its armed forces and domestic population. By 1917, widespread discontent existed in Russia.

- In 1914 Russia failed to secure a quick victory against Germany.
- Initially in 1914 the Russian army made advances and the majority of Russians supported the war.
- However, Russian forces suffered defeats against Germany at the battles of Tannenberg and Masurian Lakes.
- Poor planning and co-ordination by General Samsonov and General Rennenkampf helped cause these defeats.
- The Russians suffered approximately 230,000 casualties, far more than Germany.
- The First World War revealed the importance of new technology and tactics. The Germans were more advanced in this area than the Russian military.
- Turkey's entry into the war in November 1914 severed a key supply line for Russia into the Mediterranean.

Key developments, 1915–1917

A range of issues continued to impact on the effectiveness of the Russian armed forces.

Developments, 1915–1916

- The command centre of the Russian army (**Stavka**) was very inefficient. In 1915 transportation remained a problem and some Russian artillery units were limited to three shells per day.
- In August 1915 Russian armies retreated from Russian Poland. The Tsar dismissed his uncle, Grand Duke Nicolai, and made himself Commander-in-Chief of the Russian armed forces.
- The Tsar had limited military experience and could now be held directly responsible for further military defeats.
- The retreat resulted in 1.5 million casualties and the loss of important cities such as Vilna.

Developments, 1916–1917

- By 1916 General Alexeyev had improved the production of artillery shells and Russia still had the largest standing army of 1.7 million men.
- Alexeyev launched Russian forces against German troops around Lake Naroch in March 1916. The attack failed, causing 100,000 casualties.
- In 1916 General Brusilov launched a successful attack against Austro-Hungarian forces. However, the Russians did not have the resources to fully exploit this success.
- By December 1916, 1.6 million Russian soldiers were dead and 3.9 million were wounded.
- Many Russian generals were poor leaders and **desertions** from the Russian army increased.
- In February 1917 Russia fell into revolution and the Tsar **abdicated**.

Support or challenge?

Below is a sample exam-style question which asks how far you agree with a specific statement. Below this is a series of general statements that are relevant to the question. Using your own knowledge and the information on the opposite page decide whether these statements support or challenge the statement in the question and tick the appropriate box.

'Russia's army was doomed to fail in the First World War.' How far do you agree with this statement?

	SUPPORT	CHALLENGE
The Russians achieved a military success in the Brusilov offensive of 1916.		
The Russian armed forces experienced serious defeats at the Tannenberg and Masurian Lakes in 1914.		
General Alexeyev made some improvements in the effectiveness of the army.		
The Tsar decided to make himself Commander-in-Chief in 1915.		
The retreat from Russian Poland.		
Increased desertions from the Russian army.		
Russian army of 1.7 million men.		
Russian military leaders failed to maintain morale within the Russian army.		

Complete the paragraph

Below are a sample exam-style question and a paragraph written in answer to this question. The paragraph contains a point and specific examples, but lacks a concluding explanatory link back to the question. Complete the paragraph, adding this link in the space provided.

'The defeat of the Russian army in the First World War was inevitable.' How far do you agree with this statement?

> To a certain degree it could be argued that the defeat of the Russian Army was inevitable because it had many weaknesses. At the beginning of the First World War, even though the Russian army gained initial advances, they were soon defeated at the Battles of Tannenberg and Masurian Lakes. These defeats revealed the poor organisation and leadership of the Russian army, which supports the argument that defeat was inevitable. This is further supported by the fact that in 1915 Russian artillery was restricted to three shells per day due to economic difficulties. The Russian army also had to retreat from Russian Poland in 1915. However, in 1916 General Brusilov launched a successful attack against the Austro-Hungarians.

Section 2: Tsarism's last chance, 1906–1917

The impact of the First World War on Russian politics and economy

Revised

Political impact

In 1915 the Progressive Bloc was formed in the Duma, which consisted of different groups such as the **Kadets**. The aim of the Bloc was to convince the Tsar to establish a Ministry of Public Confidence to help run the war. The Tsar saw this as an attempt to weaken his autocratic power and he temporarily closed the Duma. He then declared himself Commander-in-Chief. This resulted in the Tsarina having greater political influence in Petrograd.

The Tsarina was German and unpopular. She appointed incompetent politicians such as Alexander Protopopov, whom she made the Minister of Internal Affairs. She also dismissed more able politicians such as the Minister of War Alexei Polivanov. She did not trust organisations such as the **Zemgor** or the **War Industries Committee**. Rasputin, a monk who helped her son Alexis with his haemophilia, influenced Alexandra. Rasputin caused national scandals by being a womaniser and drunk, which further undermined support for the Tsar. Prince Yusupov killed Rasputin in December 1916.

Strikes and protests began to occur in major cities such as Moscow and Petrograd. The Tsar ordered the strikes to be ended by force. Rodzianko, the leader of the Duma, sent telegrams requesting the return of the Tsar but was ignored. The Tsar finally decided to return to Petrograd but was prevented by striking railway workers. The country was in chaos and he had lost support of the armed forces and the Duma. On 2 March 1917 the Tsar abdicated.

Economic impact

- By 1916 the Russian economy was struggling to meet the needs of the armed forces and Russian population. Russia's finances were struggling. By 1917 inflation had reached 200 per cent.
- The Tsar had decided to ban the sale and production of alcohol during the First World War, which reduced tax revenues for the government. The country's national debt had quadrupled.
- The growth of the war economy meant more workers were needed in the cities. Between 1914 and 1917 Petrograd's population rose from 2.1 to 2.7 million.
- The rise in inflation and declining living standards resulted in labour unrest. Strikes swept across Russia towards the end of 1916 and into 1917.
- Agricultural production continued to pose a problem in the First World War. In 1916 a crisis occurred when peasants could not secure stable prices for their grain.
- Many peasants decided to hoard grain for their own use. In 1917 only 10 per cent of the total grain harvested was sold to the markets.
- Trains were being diverted for the war effort and not for transporting food to the cities. In 1914 Moscow received 2200 railway wagons of grain per month and in December 1916 it received only 300.
- Inevitably this caused severe grain shortages in the cities. In January 1917 Petrograd received only 48 per cent of its total grain requirements. The army was also forced to halve its 4000 calories per day ration.

Complex essay style

Below is a sample exam question, a list of key points to be made in the essay, and a simple introduction and conclusion for the essay. Read the question, the plan, and the introduction and conclusion. Rewrite the introduction and the conclusion in order to develop an argument.

> How far do you agree that the main consequence of the First World War in Russia was the destruction of the economy?

Key points:
- The impact of the First World War on the Tsar's authority.
- The political impact on the Duma.
- The impact of the war on the peasants and workers.
- The impact of the war on Alexandra and Rasputin.
- The impact of the war on the Russian armed forces.

Introduction

To a great extent the war did ruin the Russian economy as it caused growing tensions in the cities. The war had an impact on the Tsar's authority and the growing influence of the Tsarina and Rasputin. The war also impacted on the Duma and its relationship with the Tsar. Additionally the war caused increasing prices for goods, falling living standards and grain shortages.

Conclusion

Overall the war impacted on Russia to a significant extent. The most important impact was that it revealed the poor political leadership of the Tsar. The ruining of the economy was significant. It also revealed the agricultural problems Russia still had not resolved. The political system also failed to cope with the strains of the war and made the Tsar even more unpopular.

Identify an argument

Below are a series of definitions, a sample exam-style question and two sample conclusions. One of the conclusions achieves a high level because it contains an argument. The other achieves a lower level because it contains only description and assertion. Identify which is which. The mark scheme on page 3 will help you.

Description: a detailed account.
Assertion: a statement of fact or an opinion, which is not supported by a reason.
Reason: a statement that explains or justifies something.
Argument: an assertion justified with a reason.

> 'The main impact of the First World War was that it undermined the authority of the Tsar.' How far do you agree with this statement?

Sample 1

The main impact of the First World War was that it did undermine the authority of the Tsar to a considerable extent because the Tsar failed to rule Russia effectively after becoming Commander-in-Chief of the armed forces in 1915. The Tsarina was left in Petrograd to make important political decisions but often removed able politicians such as the Minister of War, Alexei Polivanov. Food shortages in the cities became more severe in Russia towards the end of 1916. The Duma and Russian population became more hostile to the Tsar and under pressure he abdicated in 1917. Therefore the First World War to a significant extent had a dramatic impact on the Tsar's authority.

Sample 2

The Tsar did not rule Russia effectively during the First World War. He made himself Commander-in-Chief of the armed forces in 1915, which did not help Russia. The Tsarina was left in Petrograd to make important political decisions but often removed able politicians such as the Minister of War, Alexei Polivanov. Food shortages in the cities became more severe in Russia towards the end of 1916. The Duma and Russian population became more hostile to the Tsar and under pressure he abdicated in 1917.

Section 2: Tsarism's last chance, 1906–1917

Causes of the Russian Revolution, February 1917

Revised

Background causes

- The Tsar consistently failed to deal with various social and economic problems facing Russia.
- The outbreak of the First World War made many of these problems worse, with declining living standards and food shortages.
- The army suffered horrendous casualties and military defeats.
- The Tsar made poor decisions. These included making himself Commander-in-Chief of the armed forces in 1915, and leaving the unpopular Tsarina with more political influence in Petrograd, which she failed to use effectively.

However, in January 1917 there were few indications that a revolution was imminent. The radical parties such as the Bolsheviks and Socialist Revolutionaries had not made attempts to seize power. Hence there were other events between January and March 1917 which contributed to the Tsar abdicating.

Trigger causes, January to March 1917

The February Revolution began with demonstrations and strikes in Petrograd in January 1917. On 9 January, 140,000 workers went on strike to commemorate the 'Bloody Sunday' massacre of 1905. More strikes emerged, caused by food shortages and poor working conditions. The situation was made worse when the government announced the rationing of bread on 19 February, which resulted in panic buying and further food shortages. On 23 February International Women's Day was commemorated, with thousands of women taking to the streets of Petrograd. At the same time workers from the Putilov Engineering Works went on strike.

By 25 February, 200,000 people were protesting on the streets of Petrograd. The workers established **Soviets** to put forward their demands. On 1 March the Petrograd Soviet was established and issued '**Order No. 1**', which demanded that all officers had to be elected by their soldiers.

Response of the army and government

The government	The army
The Tsar's government attempted to regain control of the city. The police arrested the leaders of the workers. All newspapers were closed down and public transport was temporarily stopped. Some troops loyal to the Tsar opened fire on protesters.	On 25 February **Cossack** troops and the elite Pavlovsky Life Guards refused to fire on demonstrators. The Tsar was losing the support of the army and his authority was being weakened. The Tsar relied heavily on the army to maintain his power. On 26 February troops from the Petrograd Garrison mutinied and joined the protesters.

The Duma

On 26 February the Tsar ordered the suspension of the Duma. The Duma established a twelve-man committee to take over the running of Russia. This committee further undermined the Tsar's authority and revealed he was losing political influence in Petrograd.

Abdication of the Tsar

On 28 February the Tsar boarded a train to Petrograd but was stopped by railway strikers. Representatives from the Duma met with the Tsar and requested his abdication. The Tsar agreed to abdicate on 2 March.

Mind map

Creating a mind map will help you answer the following question:

Why was there a revolution in Russia in February 1917?

Use the information on the opposite page to add detail to the mind map below.

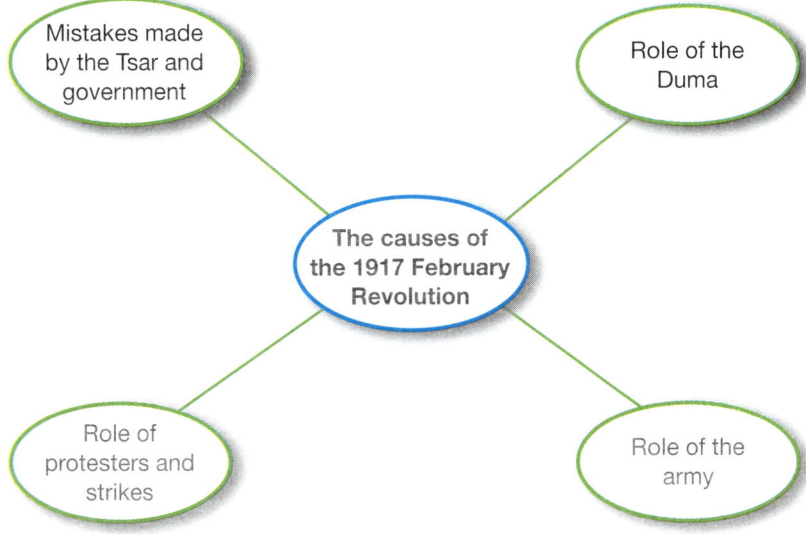

 ## Simple essay style

Below is a sample exam-style question. Use your own knowledge and the information on the opposite page to produce a plan for this question. Choose four general points, and provide three pieces of specific information to support each general point. Once you have planned your essay, write the introduction and conclusion for the essay. The introduction should list the points to be discussed in the essay. The conclusion should summarise the key points and justify which point was the most important.

How far were food shortages the key reason for revolution in Russia in February 1917?

Section 2: Tsarism's last chance, 1906–1917

The February Revolution

Key events

The causes of the revolution ranged from the mistakes of the Tsar to workers striking and the army refusing to fire on protesters. These events can be easily confused. The revolution also had some important consequences in February/March 1917. The timeline below summarises the key events in early 1917, many of which have been mentioned previously.

January	Strikes swept across Russian cities, many caused by food shortages.
14 February	100,000 workers went on strike in Petrograd.
23 February	International Women's Day encouraged further demonstrations against the Tsar.
25 February	Cossack troops failed to intervene effectively against protesters in Petrograd and protests increased.
26 February	The Tsar ordered troops to fire on protesters and some troops followed these orders. The Tsar suspended the Duma.
28 February	The Tsar attempted to return to Petrograd but was held up by striking railway workers in the town of Pskov.
1 March	The Petrograd Soviet was formed to represent the interests of the workers and issues 'Order No. 1'.
2 March	The Tsar abdicated and stated that his son would not replace him as Tsar due to his suffering from haemophilia.
3 March	The Tsar offered his throne to his brother Grand Duke Michael, but he refused. The Romanov dynasty, which had ruled Russia for more than 300 years, was now over.
3 March	Prince Lvov became the leader of the new **Provisional Government**.
March	The revolution spread across Russia. Local committees and Soviets were established, and took over responsibilities for local government.

The political situation in February 1917

The only way the Tsar could have prevented the revolution would have been to order front line troops into Petrograd to restore order and control on his behalf. However, key members of the Duma convinced important generals that they controlled events in Petrograd and that military intervention could ignite a **Civil War** within Russia. But the Duma did not fully control Petrograd. This can be seen with the establishment of the Petrograd Soviet on 1 March.

Rodzianko, one of the leading figures within the Duma, saw an opportunity to remove the Tsar. He encouraged General Nikolai Ruzsky, commander of the Northern Front, to join the Tsar at Pskov and encourage him to resign. General Alexeyev also helped to convince the Tsar to abdicate, arguing this would help the Russian war effort against Germany.

Immediate consequences of the Tsar's abdication

- Abdication increased the short-term political chaos and violence within Russia.
- Peasants began to seize land by force.
- The Duma Committee became the Provisional Government in March 1917 but did not have the support to govern effectively. The two were rivals to the growing power of the Petrograd Soviet.
- Russia was still involved in a war against Germany.

Eliminate irrelevance

Below are a sample exam-style question and a paragraph written in answer to this question. Read the paragraph and identify parts of the paragraph that are not directly relevant to the question. Draw a line through the information that is irrelevant and justify your deletions in the margin.

How far did the February revolution resolve the problems facing Russia in early 1917?

> The revolution did little to resolve the problems facing Russia. It resulted in the removal of the Tsar from power when he abdicated on 2 March 1917. The workers had carried out successful strikes throughout January 1917 and the establishment of the Petrograd Soviet in March gave them increased political influence. The Tsar made himself Commander-in-Chief in 1915 and left the unpopular Tsarina with more political influence in Petrograd. However, the extent the revolution removed all difficulties Russia faced was limited in some ways because the new Provisional Government still had to contend with the war with Germany in March 1917. The revolution had not resulted in peace. The Provisional Government continued with the war against Germany until being removed from power in October 1917 by the Bolsheviks and the problems of food shortages and lack of equipment for the Russian army were not immediately resolved. Clearly, the Provisional Government only had a limited success in resolving the problems facing Russia because they never solved the key issues of peace, land and bread.

Develop the detail

Below are a sample exam-style question and a paragraph written in answer to this question. The paragraph contains a limited amount of detail. Annotate the paragraph to add additional detail to the answer.

How far were the revolutionary events of early 1917 planned and organised?

> Describing the revolutionary events of 1917 as well planned would be inaccurate because the strikes in Russian cities were not immediately intended to bring down the Tsar. These strikes were often in response to food shortages. The streets of Petrograd saw large numbers of demonstrators in the period January to March 1917. In February some army units refused to fire on demonstrators and this was not part of a planned revolution. The Tsar failed to return to Petrograd and was convinced by close colleagues to abdicate. Therefore the extent of planning for the revolution was limited, because the Duma and army were reacting to events as they developed in the period January to March 1917.

Section 2: Tsarism's last chance, 1906–1917

Exam focus

Below is a sample A grade essay. Read it and the examiner comments around it.

> How far do you agree that the First World War was the main reason for the abdication of the Tsar in March 1917?

The candidate keeps a clear focus on 'How far' and considers differing views. The candidate includes key issues, which are developed more fully in later paragraphs.

The impact of the First World War was a very significant reason for the Tsar abdicating in March 1917, because it resulted in food shortages and millions of casualties, making many Russians hostile to the Tsar. However, there were other factors that resulted in the abdication of the Tsar. He made mistakes during the war, making his abdication more likely. The decision to appoint himself Commander-in-Chief of the armed forces in 1915 was a disaster for the Tsar.

The candidate begins the paragraph with a focused judgement and supports their argument with appropriate factual examples.

The First World War was a very important reason why the Tsar abdicated. The Russian armed forces were not always well equipped and some artillery units were limited to three shells per day. They also suffered humiliating defeats against Germany such as the Battles of Tannenberg and Masurian Lakes in 1914. The Russian army was forced into an embarrassing retreat from Russian Poland in 1915. These events did to a degree contribute to the unpopularity of the Tsar and made abdication more likely. However, his decision to make himself Commander-in-Chief of the armed forces in 1915 made him even more unpopular because he could now be held directly responsible for any future military defeats, and hence abdication became even more likely.

The candidate explores a key issue, which is a clear alternative to the given factor (the First World War) in the original question. The candidate also successfully links issues to support their arguments.

The Tsar's decision to become Commander-in-Chief was the most significant reason for his downfall. It resulted in him being away from the centre of government in Petrograd, which meant he could not resolve tensions in the critical period of January to March 1917 and this above any other factor resulted in his abdication. When he did eventually decide to return to Petrograd he was prevented by striking railway workers. This made his position more vulnerable and abdication more likely. Another impact was that he left the unpopular German Tsarina with more political influence within Petrograd. She failed to work with the Duma effectively and appointed ministers who did not openly criticise her. She even dismissed able ministers such as the Minister of War Alexei Polivanov. Rasputin, a close adviser to Alexandra, was a womaniser and a drunk and made the Tsarina and Tsar even more unpopular. The Tsar's decision to become Commander-in-Chief was the most important reason for his abdication because it removed him from the centre of power making him unable to respond to events in Petrograd.

> The War contributed to the Tsar's abdication to a considerable extent, because of its economic and social impact. By December 1916, 1.6 million Russian soldiers were dead, 3.9 million were wounded and desertions from the army increased. More people had moved to the cities to work in the factories, resulting in poorer living standards within the cities and more social discontent, especially as inflation had risen by 200 per cent by 1917. Between 1914 and 1917 Petrograd's population rose from 2.1 to 2.7 million. There were also severe food shortages in Russia by the end of 1916. In 1914 Moscow received 2200 railway wagons of grain per month and in December 1916 it received only 300. The railway wagons had been diverted to transport supplies to the Russian armed forces. Inevitably this caused severe grain shortages in the cities. In January 1917 Petrograd received only 48 per cent of its total grain requirements. Clearly, the war had a considerable impact on the Tsar's abdication because it made him very unpopular.
>
> A combination of factors resulted in the abdication of the Tsar on 2 March 1917. The First World War contributed to the Tsar's abdication to a considerable degree, especially in terms of the impact it had on the morale of the Russian population. Nonetheless, his fate was sealed when he became Commander-in-Chief. This meant that he was blamed personally for the defeats suffered in the war, whilst being removed from his capital and therefore unable to deal with the consequences of his own failure.

The candidate considers the impact of the First World War in more depth and presents alternative arguments that are supported by a range of precise facts.

The candidate recognises that a range of factors contributed to the Tsar's abdication but emphasises the role of the Tsar. Points are communicated effectively in their conclusion.

27/30
This essay would score mid-Level 5. The candidate's answer has an explicit and sustained analytical focus on 'How far'. The candidate supports their points with precise factual examples. Additionally they have linked different factors to justify their arguments. The essay has a focused introduction and conclusion. The essay is well structured and points have been communicated clearly.

Changing focus

This essay argues that the most important reason for the Tsar's abdication was his decision to appoint himself Commander-in-Chief. But the essay also considers a range of other factors. Pick one of these other factors and rewrite the introduction, the conclusion and the relevant paragraph, arguing that this factor was the most important.

Section 3: February to October 1917

Difficulties facing the Provisional Government

Immediate problems

The **Provisional Government** membership consisted mainly of the **Octobrist** and **Kadet** parties. These parties did not have popular support throughout Russia.

- The government did not include members from the **Mensheviks** or **Bolsheviks**. This meant that these groups helped to form a rival power base in the Petrograd government. This system became known as dual government, which made it more difficult to make clear decisions and create effective government.
- They allowed more political freedoms and this meant people were allowed to criticise the government more openly.
- In June 1917, the Petrograd **Soviet** became the All-Russia Soviet and also claimed the right to issue laws for Russia. They issued '**Order No. 1**', which undermined the authority of military officers. It stated that the military orders of the Provisional Government should only be followed if agreed by the Petrograd Soviet.
- The Soviet was dominated by **left-wing** political groups such as the **Socialist Revolutionaries** and Bolsheviks, and became rivals to the Provisional Government.
- Major decisions in theory had to be agreed by both the Provisional Government and the Petrograd Soviet, but this did not encourage decisive and efficient government, which Russia desperately needed in 1917.

Impact of the First World War, March to October 1917

Britain and France informed the Provisional Government that they would continue to loan Russia money as long as Russia stayed in the war against Germany. Some members of the Provisional Government believed it was Russia's duty to stay in the war. The Russian Foreign Minister Paul Milyukov argued that Russia's future was with the democratic nations of France and Britain.

Initially Russian military morale improved after the Tsar's abdication, but poor supplies and continued economic problems reversed this process. In March 1917 the Soviet declared that they would only support a defensive war against Germany. The Provisional Government hoped to regain lost territory and expand Russia's borders after gaining victory. In April 1917 demonstrations against the war became more frequent in Petrograd.

Role of Alexander Kerensky

In order to win support domestically and internationally, the Provisional Government supported the 'June Offensive' against the Austro-Hungarian army. The offensive failed, mass **desertions** from the Russian army increased and morale began to collapse. In July riots and protests against the war increased across Russia, especially in Petrograd. Kerensky, a member of the Socialist Revolutionary Party who had connections in both the Provisional Government and the Petrograd Soviet, became the new Prime Minister in July 1917. He failed to resolve the problems facing Russia.

Developments in rural Russia

The Provisional Government exerted control in major cities such as Moscow, but their influence in the countryside was limited. Some peasants began to seize land from large landowners. The Provisional Government did not have the capability to prevent such seizures of land. Political, social and economic chaos was increasing in the countryside. The army at this point could not be relied upon to restore order across Russia.

RAG – Rate the timeline

Below are a sample exam-style question and a timeline. Read the question, study the timeline and, using three coloured pens, put a Red, Amber or Green star next to the events to show:

Red: Events and policies that have no relevance to the question.

Amber: Events and policies that have some significance to the question.

Green: Events and policies that are directly relevant to the question.

1. How far did the Provisional Government successfully deal with the problems they faced in the period March to July 1917?

Now repeat the activity with the following questions.

2. How far do you agree that the problems faced by the Provisional Government in the period March to July 1917 could not be solved?

3. Why did the Provisional Government not act more decisively in the period March to July 1917?

Spectrum of significance

Below are a sample exam-style question and a list of general points which could be used to answer the question. Use your own knowledge and the information on the opposite page to reach a judgement about the importance of these general points to the question posed. Write numbers on the spectrum below to indicate their relative importance. Having done this, write a brief justification of your placement, explaining why some of these factors are more important than others. The resulting diagram could form the basis of an essay plan.

> How far did the Provisional Government successfully deal with the problems they faced in the period March to July 1917?

1. Pressure placed by Britain and France on the Provisional Government to stay in the war.
2. The relationship between the Provisional Government and the Petrograd Soviet.
3. Morale in the Russian army.
4. Controlling the countryside.
5. Dealing with political opposition.
6. Solving Russia's social and economic problems.

⟵―――――――――――――――――――――――――⟶

Very successfully   Not very successfully

33

Section 3: February to October 1917

The impact of Lenin's return to Russia in April 1917

Lenin's background

Lenin supported Marxism. Karl Marx argued that industrialisation had resulted in a growing working class who were exploited by the **bourgeoisie**, who would be removed by a revolution of the **proletariat**. After the revolution, a socialist society would emerge based on equality, which would evolve into **communism**. Lenin realised the majority of Russia's population were peasants and an industrial working-class revolution across Russia was impossible. Lenin argued that the revolution would need to be led by small group of disciplined revolutionaries. His views caused a split in the Russian Social Democrat Party in 1903. Lenin's party, the Bolsheviks, provided the elite leadership for any future revolution. Arguably, without Lenin there would not have been a communist revolution in October 1917.

Lenin's return from exile

Lenin had not expected the abdication of the Tsar in March 1917. He had been living in exile in Zurich, Switzerland. The German government supported Lenin's return to Russia on 3 April 1917 because he opposed Russia's involvement in the First World War.

The April Theses

When Lenin arrived in Petrograd by train, he demanded an immediate social revolution. Lenin produced a document known as the April Theses. In this document he made a clear promise of 'Peace, Land and Bread'; he also declared 'All Power to the Soviets'. Lenin's declarations were designed to gain support for the Bolsheviks.

Many Russians opposed the war with Germany, therefore the promise of 'Peace, Land and Bread' attracted the support of some. Lenin emphasised the failure of the Provisional Government to redistribute land to the peasants. He argued the Provisional Government was too influenced by the middle classes and wealthy landowners. Lenin argued that the Soviets should govern Russia and the Provisional Government should be removed.

Lenin's impact

- On 21 April Lenin sent Bolsheviks to factories in Petrograd to gain support for strikes, in an attempt to remove the Provisional Government from power.
- The Bolsheviks had a limited impact, and there were no mass strikes.
- Many Russian Marxists believed Russia was not ready for a communist revolution in 1917.
- Lenin's leadership skills remained a threat to the Provisional Government.

The June Offensive

Arguably, before the July Days the Bolshevik Party had made little progress in gaining power. It had an active membership of only 10,000. However, when the Provisional Government supported the ill-fated offensive against Austro-Hungarian forces in June, support for the Bolsheviks grew. The Bolsheviks benefited from not collaborating with the Provisional Government before the failure of the June Offensive.

The impact of the June Offensive

The Provisional Government and Petrograd Soviet saw the Bolsheviks as a threat. Troops remained loyal to the government and the Bolshevik attempt to gain power failed. However, their popularity amongst the workers and within the cities began to grow.

Complete the paragraph

Below are a sample exam-style question and a paragraph written in answer to this question. The paragraph contains a point and specific examples, but lacks a concluding explanatory link back to the question. Complete the paragraph, adding this link in the space provided.

How far did Lenin's return to Russia in 1917 weaken and threaten the Provisional Government?

> Lenin's return to Russia weakened the Provisional Government to a significant extent because he provided the Bolsheviks with clear leadership, which posed a threat to the government. His April Theses emphasised the promise of 'Peace, Land and Bread'. He realised that many Russians opposed the continuation of the war against Germany and the decision by the Provisional Government not to seek peace. He also knew that many people viewed the Provisional Government as being dominated by landowners and the middle classes. Lenin also promised 'All Power to the Soviets', which was a popular message. However, he did not attract the mass support of the Russian people in April 1917 and there were other important factors which weakened and threatened the Provisional Government.

Turning assertion into argument

Below are a sample exam-style question and a series of assertions. Read the question and then add a justification to each of the assertions to turn it into an argument.

How far did Lenin's return to Russia in April 1917 weaken and threaten the Provisional Government?

> Lenin's return to Russia to a certain extent threatened the government in the sense that
>
> Lenin's promise of 'Peace, Land and Bread' was important in weakening the government to a certain degree in the sense that
>
> The significance of Lenin's return to Russia in April 1917 should not be over-emphasised and other factors to a considerable degree threatened the government in the sense that

Section 3: February to October 1917

The significance of the July Days and General Kornilov

The July Days

The July Days occurred between 3 July and 6 July and saw demonstrations in Petrograd and across Russia. These demonstrations were caused by the failure of the June Offensive, continued food shortages and continued economic chaos within Russia. The soldiers and sailors from the **Kronstadt naval base** organised an armed demonstration with the aim of causing the collapse of the Provisional Government. They protested outside the Marinsky Palace, which was the headquarters of the Provisional Government. At the height of the protests on 4 July 50,000 people surrounded the Tauride Palace, the headquarters of the Soviet, awaiting directions on how to proceed. Many of the demonstrators looked to the Bolsheviks for clear leadership but Lenin failed to fully exploit the situation.

> #### The end of the Bolshevik threat?
> The Provisional Government and members of the Petrograd Soviet saw the Bolsheviks as a threat to their own power. Whilst the Bolsheviks did not have a majority in the Petrograd Soviet, the July Days showed that their popularity was growing.
>
> In order to deal with the Bolsheviks, the Provisional Government and the Soviet appealed for workers not to continue with the protests. They also brought in loyal troops from outside of Petrograd to restore order. On 6 July soldiers surrounded the Bolshevik headquarters at Kshesinskaia Mansion and 500 Bolsheviks inside surrendered. The demonstrations collapsed and Lenin was accused of being a German spy and was forced to escape to Finland. At this point the Bolshevik threat to the Provisional Government appeared to be over. After the July Days, Lenin feared he had missed his opportunity to seize power.

The Kornilov Affair

After the mass desertions from the Russian army caused by the failed June Offensive, Kerensky replaced Prince Lvov as Prime Minister and brought back the death penalty. General Kornilov became the new Commander-in-Chief, replacing General Brusilov. The actual events of the Kornilov Revolt are not clear. Kornilov decided to march on Petrograd on 24 August with reliable troops, to restore order on behalf of the Provisional Government. Kerensky thought Kornilov was also going to remove him from power. He decided to provide weapons to the **Red Guards** and released Bolsheviks from prison, supplying them with weapons. Kornilov realised he had been betrayed by Kerensky and continued to march on Petrograd, but lost the support of his troops and was arrested on 1 September.

Consequences of the revolt

- The Kornilov Affair seriously weakened the Provisional Government.
- Support for the All-Russia Soviet was increased.
- Kerensky lost the support of both the right- and left-wing political parties.
- Discipline within the Russian armed forces deteriorated even further.
- These events created a power vacuum. This provided Lenin and the Bolsheviks, who now had more weapons, with an opportunity to seize power.
- The Bolsheviks won a majority of support in the Petrograd Soviet.

Delete as applicable

Below is a sample exam-style question and a paragraph written in answer to this question. Read the paragraph and decide which of the possible options (in bold) is most appropriate. Delete the least appropriate options and complete the paragraph by justifying your selection.

> How far was Kerensky responsible for weakening the Provisional Government in the period June to October 1917?

Kerensky was responsible to a **great/fair/limited** extent for weakening the Provisional Government in 1917. For example, he did not end Russia's involvement in the First World War when he became Prime Minister in July 1917 after the July Days protests in Petrograd. He knew how unpopular the June Offensive against Austria–Hungary had been within Russia and that morale within the Russian armed forces was on the verge of collapse. He initially supported the appointment of General Kornilov becoming Commander-in-Chief of the Russian armed forces. Hence when Kornilov marched on Petrograd on 24 August, Kerensky was responsible for weakening the Provisional Government to a **large/moderate/small** degree because

_____
_____

Develop the detail

Below are a sample exam-style question and a paragraph written in answer to this question. The paragraph contains a limited amount of detail. Annotate the paragraph to add additional detail to the answer.

> How far was the Kornilov Affair the main reason for the failure of the Provisional Government in 1917?

General Kornilov's coup weakened the Provisional Government to a large extent. His decision helped Lenin and the Bolsheviks. The Provisional Government's Prime Minister did not make wise choices when he discovered that Kornilov was marching on Petrograd. Furthermore, the coup affected the popularity of the government and the Bolsheviks. In this way, Kornilov's coup was an extremely important factor in explaining the failure of the Provisional Government because it both weakened the government and helped the opposition.

Section 3: February to October 1917

The key events of the October 1917 Revolution

Important steps before October 1917

- After the July Days Lenin placed more emphasis on his message of 'Peace, Land and Bread', which gained the Bolsheviks more support from the workers and peasants.
- The Kornilov Revolt convinced many workers that the Russian military leaders were planning a military dictatorship.
- Lenin also encouraged the establishment of 41 Bolshevik newspapers across Russia to spread his message.
- Importantly, the Bolsheviks had established the **Red Guards** and they had gained weapons from Kerensky during the Kornilov Revolt.
- In August the Provisional Government announced that elections would take place for a new **Constituent Assembly** in November. Lenin knew that the Bolsheviks would not do as well as the Socialist Revolutionaries in these elections. He was determined to seize power before November.
- By the end of September the Bolsheviks dominated the Petrograd Soviet and Lenin continued to demand 'All Power to the Soviets'.
- Lenin secretly returned to Petrograd on 10 October and eventually persuaded the **Bolshevik Central Committee** to support an armed seizure of power in Petrograd. However, Zinoviev and Kamenev remained opposed to the seizure of power and advocated a coalition government.

Role of Trotsky

Lenin gave responsibility for the **coup** to Leon Trotsky, a former leading Social Democrat who had only joined the Bolsheviks in May. On 25 September Trotsky was elected the chairman of the Petrograd Soviet. He was placed in charge of the **Military Revolutionary Committee** of the Petrograd Soviet. Trotsky devised the plan, which resulted in the successful take-over of power in Petrograd on 25 and 26 October.

Key events in the Revolution

The Military Revolutionary Committee

On 24 October the Provisional Government attempted to close two Bolshevik newspapers within Petrograd. After this Lenin authorised Trotsky to begin the take-over of power. Trotsky intended to use the Military Revolutionary Committee to take over Petrograd on 26 October and he would claim he had acted on behalf of the Petrograd Soviet.

Storming the Winter Palace

During the evening of 24 October the Red Guards occupied important areas and buildings within Petrograd. Soldiers who had previously served the Provisional Government offered little resistance. Trotsky and the Red Guards successfully arrested the majority of the Provisional Government, who were based in the Winter Palace. The Winter Palace was defended by female troops and trainee officer cadets, hence resistance was limited. On 25 October the Military Revolutionary Committee announced that the Provisional Government had been 'deposed'. Kerensky fled Petrograd with the support of the American Embassy and hoped to gain the support of loyal troops to crush the Bolsheviks.

The All-Russia Soviet

Delegates from the All-Russia Soviet met during the evening of 25 October at the Smolny Institute. Lenin knew the Bolsheviks dominated the All-Russia Soviet. The Bolsheviks had 390 seats whilst the Mensheviks only had 80 seats and the Socialist Revolutionaries 180 seats. Therefore the All-Russia Soviet supported the removal of the Provisional Government by the Bolsheviks. Now Lenin and the Bolsheviks had to consolidate their power across all of Russia.

Spot the mistake

Below are a sample exam-style question and a paragraph written in answer to this question. Why does this paragraph not get into Level 4? Once you have identified the mistake, rewrite the paragraph so that it displays the qualities of Level 4. The mark scheme on page 3 will help you.

> How accurate is it to say that Trotsky's role ensured the success of the Bolshevik Revolution of 1917?

> Trotsky joined the Bolshevik party in May 1917. He became Chairman of the Petrograd Soviet and took over the running of the Military Revolutionary Committee. Trotsky helped plan the October Revolution and was supported by Lenin. Trotsky's supporters took control of the Winter Palace and arrested members of the Provisional Government. The leader of the Provisional Government fled Petrograd as he had lost support of the armed forces within the city.

Delete as applicable

Below are a sample exam-style question and a paragraph written in answer to this question. Read the paragraph and decide which of the possible options (in bold) is most appropriate. Delete the least appropriate options and complete the paragraph by justifying your selection.

> How significant was Lenin's role in the overthrow of the Provisional Government in 1917?

> Lenin's role was significant to a **great/fair/limited** extent because he convinced the Bolsheviks to seize power after he returned to Petrograd on 10 October. The Central Committee was split on the question of a second revolution. Some leading Bolsheviks such as Kamenev and Zinoviev opposed Lenin's demands and called for a coalition government. However, Lenin was able to persuade the majority of the central committee to back his plan for a revolution. Lenin was important to a **great/considerable/limited** degree because

Section 3: February to October 1917

The extent of Bolshevik support in October 1917

Impact of the Provisional Government

Within Petrograd there was little support for the Provisional Government. They had failed to deal with the problems of food shortages and redistribution of land. Kerensky managed to gain some support from **Cossack** soldiers who advanced on Petrograd on 28 October. The Red Guards defeated the Cossacks. However, the success of the Bolsheviks and the unpopularity of the Provisional Government did not mean that Lenin had widespread support across all of Russia.

Bolshevik support

Support in Petrograd/major cities	Support in the countryside
<ul><li>The Provisional Government failed to significantly improve working conditions in factories within Russian cities such as Petrograd.</li><li>As the economy declined, workers increased their demands.</li><li>Rising prices and food shortages resulted in more frequent strikes, especially after the July Days of 1917.</li><li>In this context, workers were becoming more radical and the promises of the Bolsheviks became more appealing.</li><li>However, many workers would have supported any party that promised to resolve their problems and improve the economy. If the Provisional Government and the Soviets failed to solve these problems then Lenin and the Bolsheviks might have the answers. It was in this context that support for the Bolsheviks grew in major cities such as Petrograd, which was also the centre of political power.</li><li>In February 1917 membership of the Bolshevik Party numbered 10,000. By September 1917 this had increased to 300,000.</li><li>However, this still does not mean the majority of the Russian population supported the Bolsheviks.</li></ul>	<ul><li>The vast majority of the Russian population in 1917 were still peasants.</li><li>During 1917 there was an increasing number of peasants using violence against landlords and forcibly seizing land.</li><li>The Provisional Government was losing support, as it had done in the cities.</li><li>The most popular political party amongst the peasants was the Socialist Revolutionaries, who focused many of their policies on meeting the demands of the peasants, such as the redistribution of land.</li><li>Lenin knew that the Socialist Revolutionaries would gain more electoral support in the proposed constituent elections of November 1917.</li><li>Bolshevik support was more concentrated in the cities amongst the industrial working class whose numbers were far less than the peasants.</li><li>However, by October 1917 more peasants were becoming disillusioned with the Socialist Revolutionaries and Mensheviks, who were more closely linked to the Provisional Government than the Bolsheviks.</li></ul>

Support in the army

After the Kornilov Affair, relations between the army and Provisional Government further deteriorated. By October 1917 many soldiers were refusing to take orders and were becoming more radical in their demands. The Russian army was collapsing and the Provisional Government's power was evaporating. However, this does not mean the majority of soldiers immediately turned towards supporting the Bolsheviks. Instead, when the Bolsheviks seized power in October 1917, they presented themselves as an effective alternative to the failed Provisional Government, which gained them more support.

Identify an argument

Below are a series of definitions, a sample exam-style question and two sample conclusions. One of the conclusions achieves a high level because it contains an argument. The other achieves a lower level because it contains only description and assertion. Identify which is which. The mark scheme on page 3 will help you.

Description: a detailed account.
Assertion: a statement of fact or an opinion that is not supported by a reason.
Reason: a statement that explains or justifies something.
Argument: an assertion justified with a reason.

How accurate is the view that the Bolsheviks had widespread support across Russia in 1917?

Sample 1

The view that the Bolsheviks had widespread support across Russia is not completely accurate, because Russians supported different groups. The Socialist Revolutionaries in October 1917 had considerable support in the countryside, even though some peasants were becoming disillusioned with this party due to their close association with the Provisional Government. Bolshevik support tended to be concentrated in the cities amongst the industrial working classes, who were not as numerous as the peasants. In October 1917 Bolshevik support was increasing due to Lenin's promise of 'Peace, Land and Bread', but to say the majority of Russians supported the Bolsheviks would not be valid.

Sample 2

Lenin promised 'Peace, Land and Bread' to the Russian population to attract support. The Provisional Government had failed to solve the problems of food shortages in the cities and failed to redistribute land to the peasants, which made them more unpopular. The Bolsheviks were not the only left-wing political group who sought the support of the Russian population in 1917. Importantly, the Bolsheviks had effective leaders such as Lenin and Trotsky.

Spot the mistake

Below are a sample exam-style question and a paragraph written in answer to this question. Why does this paragraph not get into Level 4? Once you have identified the mistake, rewrite the paragraph so that it displays the qualities of Level 4. The mark scheme on page 3 will help you.

How far were the Bolsheviks successful in attracting widespread support across Russia in October 1917?

The Bolsheviks were to a certain extent successful in attracting support because they had an effective leader. He made important promises, which gained more support from Russians in 1917. The Bolshevik leadership also successfully exploited the mistakes made by the Provisional Government to gain more support. However, there were other political parties that also had a considerable amount of support in Russia in October 1917.

Section 3: February to October 1917

Why did the Bolsheviks succeed in October 1917?

Role of Lenin

In February 1917 the Bolshevik party was the least likely party to take power. Leading Bolsheviks such as Kamenev and Stalin supported the Provisional Government before Lenin's return in April 1917. A key factor for Bolshevik success is that Lenin seized the opportunity in October 1917. When he returned to Russia on 10 October it took him until 18 October to convince the Bolshevik Central Committee to support the idea of taking power by force. Even then, leading Bolsheviks such as Kamenev and Zinoviev still opposed such a move. Additionally, allowing Trotsky to organise the planned take-over was an astute move because Trotsky had only just joined the Bolsheviks from the Social Democratic Party and he had influence within the Petrograd Soviet. Trotsky organised the take-over of power very efficiently and with minimum force.

Weaknesses of the other parties

- The Kadets dominated the Provisional Government but failed to attract the support of the majority of Russians and had limited support amongst the workers within the cities.
- The peasants and the workers often viewed the Kadets as serving the interests of the propertied classes.
- The Mensheviks had widespread support amongst the workers and the Socialist Revolutionaries had considerable support amongst the Peasants. However, in contrast to the Bolsheviks, neither party's leadership developed a clear strategy to gain power.
- After the July Days, the Mensheviks and Socialist Revolutionaries were more closely linked to the actions of the Provisional Government. The Bolsheviks seemed less connected to the government, and their support began to increase amongst the workers and some soldiers. However, their support amongst the peasants remained weak.
- A crucial mistake made by the Mensheviks was not to support the creation of a Soviet Government after the July Days. Their support deteriorated rapidly, whilst support for the Bolsheviks increased.

The fall of the Provisional Government

It must be emphasised that the Kornilov Affair and Kerensky's decision to provide the Red Guards with weapons and release Bolshevik prisoners gave Lenin the momentum, opportunity and means to seize power. This further weakened the Provisional Government and Kerensky, and made the Bolsheviks appear politically stronger. Since coming to power in February 1917 the Provisional Government had consistently failed to resolve various problems such as food shortages, redistribution of land, high inflation and the war. The decision to launch the June Offensive convinced many Russians that the Provisional Government could not be trusted and should be replaced.

> ### Lenin and the Soviets
> The Soviets were the only real alternative as a political power base, and Lenin successfully manipulated events in October 1917 to provide the impression that it was the Soviets that were taking over power. In reality, Lenin had taken the first steps towards establishing a communist dictatorship. The other political parties such as the Socialist Revolutionaries failed to prevent this from happening in October 1917.

Complex essay style

Below are a sample exam-style question, a list of key points to be made in the essay, and a simple introduction and conclusion for the essay. Read the question, the plan, and the introduction and conclusion. Rewrite the introduction and the conclusion in order to develop an argument.

Why did the Bolsheviks succeed in October 1917 whilst other political parties failed to gain power?

Key points:
- The role of Lenin.
- The role of Trotsky.
- Weaknesses of other political parties.
- Mistakes made by the Provisional Government and Kerensky.

Introduction

A range of reasons resulted in the Bolsheviks taking power in October 1917. These were the roles of Lenin and Trotsky, the weaknesses of other political parties and mistakes made by the Provisional Government and Kerensky.

Conclusion

A range of reasons resulted in the Bolsheviks taking power in October 1917. The most important reason was the leadership of Lenin. He performed a more significant role than all of the other factors.

Eliminate irrelevance

Below are a sample exam-style question and a paragraph written in answer to this question. Read the paragraph and identify parts of the paragraph that are not directly relevant to the question. Draw a line through the information that is irrelevant and justify your deletions in the margin.

Why did the Bolsheviks succeed in October 1917 whilst other political parties failed to gain power?

The Bolsheviks were successful in taking power because other parties failed to exploit the weakness of the Provisional Government in October 1917. The Tsar had always been unpopular and so had his German wife Alexandra. The Provisional Government was also unpopular, especially after the failure of the June Offensive. After the July Days the Mensheviks and Socialist Revolutionaries were closely associated with the Provisional Government and this weakened their support, whilst support for the Bolsheviks increased, especially within the cities. This partially explains why the Bolsheviks were successful. Additionally, Lenin managed to convince the Bolshevik Central Committee to support an armed take-over of power whilst other political parties such as the Socialist Revolutionaries were not so decisive. After gaining power, Lenin began to secure his regime and launched the Red Terror, supported by the Cheka, to secure his political power. Therefore, the Bolsheviks were successful in gaining power in October because Lenin successfully exploited the weaknesses of the Provisional Government.

Section 3: February to October 1917

Exam focus

Below is a sample A grade essay. Read it and the examiner comments around it.

Why did the Bolsheviks succeed in taking power in October 1917?

The introduction reveals a clear understanding of the question. It reveals a very good awareness of the historical context and begins to consider causal significance.

In February 1917 no one would have expected the Bolsheviks to take political power by October 1917. The active membership of the Bolsheviks was only 10,000 people. They were less popular than parties such as the Mensheviks and Socialist Revolutionaries. Some leading Bolsheviks such as Kamenev even supported the Provisional Government in February 1917. However, this all changed with the return of Lenin to Russia in April 1917 and he performed a crucial role in the Bolsheviks seizing power in October 1917.

A key reason the Bolsheviks succeeded in October 1917 was due to Lenin's return to Russia in April 1917. He issued his famous April Theses, which contained his promise of 'Peace, Land and Bread'. This message became more and more popular throughout 1917, especially amongst the workers in the cities, and this partly explains why the Bolsheviks were successful in October 1917. However, this promise would not have been so powerful if the Provisional Government had not consistently made serious mistakes, such as failing to resolve the problem of food shortages, high inflation and the redistribution of land. Lenin's return to Russia helped the Bolsheviks gain power because his slogans were attractive when the Provisional Government started to fail.

The role of the Provisional Government is significant in understanding why Lenin and the Bolsheviks came to power in October 1917. Not only did they fail to resolve serious political problems, they arguably made the situation worse. In June 1917 the Provisional Government supported a large-scale offensive against the Austro-Hungarians, which ended in failure. The majority of Russians wanted to fight a defensive war. This event led to the July Days, which saw widespread protests, strikes and increased desertions from the Russian army. Interestingly, Lenin failed to exploit these events fully and was even branded a traitor and had to flee Russia. However, Kerensky came to power as Prime Minister and General Kornilov replaced General Brusilov as Commander-in-Chief of the armed forces. The failings of the Provisional Government also helped the Bolsheviks seize power because they made the government unpopular and people turned to the Bolsheviks as a result.

The candidate has included very precise facts to support and develop their arguments.

44

Kornilov was a significant factor in the Bolsheviks gaining power. Towards the end of August, Kornilov ordered his forces to march on Petrograd to restore order. Kerensky viewed this as a military attempt to take over the government of Russia. Kerensky decided to release Bolshevik prisoners and provide weapons to the Red Guards to prevent Kornilov from taking the city. Kornilov failed to reach the city as railway workers refused to transport his soldiers to the city and many of his men deserted. Within Petrograd there were now thousands of armed Bolsheviks who posed a serious threat to the Provisional Government and this was a factor in Lenin eventually gaining power in October 1917. Kornilov's coup helped the Bolsheviks gain power because it forced the Provisional Government to arm the Bolsheviks.

Lenin's return to Russia on 10 October was another reason why the Bolsheviks successfully took power. He convinced the Bolshevik Central Committee to support an armed take-over even though some leading Bolsheviks such as Kamenev and Zinoviev opposed this action. Lenin also made the crucial decision to appoint Trotsky to organise the planned take-over. He had just joined the Bolsheviks in May from the Social Democrats and had influence within the Petrograd Soviet. When Trotsky's plan was implemented between 24 and 25 October it appeared to be a Soviet take-over and this reduced opposition. The take-over was very efficient with the minimum loss of life. Lenin's return was important because he persuaded the Central Committee to seize power.

The candidate extends the range by mentioning another factor relevant to the question.

Throughout 1917 events unfolded which contributed to Lenin and the Bolsheviks taking power. The reason they succeeded was mainly due to the decisions made by Lenin during the period April to October 1917. Mistakes made by the Provisional Government such as the June Offensive and freeing political prisoners in March 1917 created the circumstances that Lenin could exploit to gain power successfully. Fortunately for Lenin the other major left-wing parties such as the Socialist Revolutionaries failed to exploit these events as effectively, and this was crucial in the Bolshevik success in October 1917.

The candidate reaches a clear conclusion, communicating their points effectively.

24/30

This essay would gain top Level 4. The candidate's analysis is explicit and not implicit. They have developed their arguments with precise factual examples. Additionally they have explored a range of issues and explained why Lenin's role was the most important factor. The candidate has also explored causal significance. The answer is well structured and points have been communicated clearly. The candidate reaches a clear conclusion.

Moving from Level 4 to Level 5

The Exam Focus at the end of Section 1 (pages 16–17) provided a Level 5 essay. The essay here achieves a Level 4. Read both essays, and the examiner's comments provided. Make a list of the additional features required to push a Level 4 essay into Level 5.

Section 4:
Keeping and consolidating power, 1918–1924

Establishment of the Sovnarkom and closing of the Constituent Assembly

Immediate challenges facing Lenin

Once the **Bolsheviks** had taken power, Lenin had to form a government. Lenin faced various problems:

- The continuing war with Germany.
- Peasants continued to seize land across Russia and the economy was in chaos.
- The Bolsheviks had substantial support within the cities but their support was still limited in the countryside.
- The Bolsheviks faced strikes by **civil servants** who refused to co-operate with the new government.
- The State Bank refused to provide the Bolsheviks with financial support.
- Finally, Lenin knew the Bolsheviks would not perform as well as the **Socialist Revolutionaries** in the forthcoming elections to the **Constituent Assembly**.

Lenin passed different **decrees** through the All-Russia **Soviet** to help overcome these difficulties and gain more support from the population:

- The Decree on Land which redistributed land to all peasants.
- The Peace Decree that emphasised that the Bolsheviks were seeking an immediate end to Russia's role in the First World War.
- The decree that established a new government organisation.

Establishment of the Sovnarkom

At the top of the new government was the **Sovnarkom**, which was a Council of People's **Commissars**. Lenin acted as the chairman of this group and was the overall leader of the new government. Below the Sovnarkom was the All-Russia Congress of Soviets, which the Bolsheviks dominated. At the bottom of this new government organisation were representatives from cities, villages and local Soviets.

> #### The purpose of Sovnarkom
> This new system of government was designed to allow the Bolsheviks to extend their power and control across Russia. Lenin and leading Bolsheviks would decide who was included in the Sovnarkom and therefore what important decisions would be made.

Closing of the Constituent Assembly

Lenin did not feel secure enough in late October to cancel the elections to the Constituent Assembly scheduled for 12 November. The elections revealed that the Bolsheviks only had the support of a quarter of the Russian population. The Socialist Revolutionaries, with a large peasant vote, became the largest party within the Constituent Assembly and gained 40.4 per cent of the vote. The Bolsheviks gained 24 per cent and was the second largest party.

Bolshevik strengths:

- They had considerable support on the northern and western military fronts.
- They had support in the military districts in Petrograd and Moscow.
- The Baltic fleet and Kronstadt Sailors also supported the Bolsheviks.
- Approximately 10 million people had voted for them.
- Opposition parties such as the **Mensheviks** and Socialist Revolutionaries were divided and failed to effectively oppose the Bolsheviks.
- Lenin managed to form a coalition with **left-wing** Socialist Revolutionaries.

The Constituent Assembly only met once, on 5 January. Lenin demanded that the Constituent Assembly should be subservient to the Sovnarkom and Soviet. The members of the Constituent Assembly rejected this demand by a vote of 237 to 137. Lenin then used the **Red Guards** to close down the Constituent Assembly and hopes for democracy were ended.

Support or challenge?

Below is a sample exam-style question, which asks how far you agree with a specific statement. Below this are a series of general statements, which are relevant to the question. Using your own knowledge and the information on the opposite page decide whether these statements support or challenge the statement in the question and tick the appropriate box.

How significant was Lenin in maintaining Bolshevik power in the period November 1917 to January 1918?

	SUPPORT	CHALLENGE
Sovnarkom was established.		
The Red Guards closed down the Constituent Assembly.		
A coalition with some Socialist Revolutionaries was arranged.		
The Mensheviks were divided and did not oppose Lenin effectively, which helped the Bolsheviks stay in power.		
Divisions within the Socialist Revolutionaries helped the Bolsheviks stay in power.		

Delete as applicable

Below are a sample exam-style question and a paragraph written in answer to this question. Read the paragraph and decide which of the possible options (in bold) is most appropriate. Delete the least appropriate options and complete the paragraph by justifying your selection.

How significant was Lenin in maintaining Bolshevik power in the period November 1917 to January 1918?

> Lenin was significant to a **great/fair/limited** extent because he made some very important decisions. He passed three decrees to secure the position of the Bolsheviks. These decrees supported ending the war, redistributing land to the peasants and establishing a new government organisation. These decrees were designed to gain more support for the Bolsheviks and strengthen their power. The establishment of the Sovnarkom provided Lenin with a clear power base from which key decisions could be made to secure power for the Bolsheviks. In this way, Lenin was very important to a **considerable/certain/limited** extent because

Section 4: Keeping and consolidating power, 1918–1924

Early measures to secure Communist control and establishment of the Police State

Revised

Treaty of Brest-Litovsk, March 1918

Lenin was determined to end the war, and knew it had been a key reason for the collapse of the Tsar's regime and the **Provisional Government**. The war remained very unpopular and Lenin needed to utilise his military resources to secure the power of the Bolsheviks, not to fight against the Germans. Lenin appointed Trotsky to conduct the peace negotiations with the Germans in the town of Brest-Litovsk. The German demands were very harsh. They demanded:

- the Baltic States, which included Latvia, Lithuania and Estonia
- Poland
- the Ukraine, an important agricultural region.

The above meant that Russia would lose:

- 32 per cent of its arable land
- 26 per cent of its railway system
- 33 per cent of its factories
- 75 per cent of its coal and iron ore mines
- approximately 60 million Russian citizens.

Many Bolsheviks opposed the peace agreement, including Trotsky, who declared 'neither peace nor war'. Lenin convinced them to agree. On 3 March 1918 Trotsky signed the Treaty of Brest-Litovsk. The Bolsheviks had paid a high price for peace but Lenin knew it would help him secure his power within Russia.

The Cheka

The secret police known as the **Cheka** was established in December 1917. Felix Dzerzhinsky was the first Head of the Cheka and its headquarters were in the Lubyanka in Moscow. Initially, they focused on ending strikes by government workers. They were also used to eliminate political opponents of the Bolsheviks and to shoot deserters from the Red Army. After a failed assassination attempt on Lenin in 1918, the Cheka launched what became known as the 'Red Terror'. Anybody who criticised the government could be arrested, and many people were shot without trial.

As time progressed, the Cheka was also used to check on the loyalty of party members. It operated outside of Soviet or party control and was used to spread fear. In later years the Cheka changed its name to the OGPU, NKVD and KGB.

Other policies

The Bolsheviks continued to allow peasants to seize land and workers were allowed to take over factories in the first six months of Bolshevik rule. This was not official government policy, but in the first few months the government did not have the capability to exert control across all of Russia.

The Bolsheviks also implemented the following:

- a Supreme Economic Council to help restore Russia's economy
- **nationalisation** of the banks
- banning of the **Kadet** political party
- establishment of the Red Army
- establishment of revolutionary tribunals to try political enemies
- ending of all foreign and domestic debts.

Despite all these measures, after six months the Bolsheviks were struggling to exert control over Russia. By May 1918, Russia was descending into **Civil War**.

Spot the mistake

Below are a sample exam-style question and a paragraph written in answer to this question. Why does this paragraph not get into Level 4? Once you have identified the mistake, rewrite the paragraph so that it displays the qualities of Level 4. The mark scheme on page 3 will help you.

> How far do you agree that the Red Terror was the main way in which the Bolsheviks consolidated their power prior to the outbreak of the Civil War?

> The Red Terror was the main way in which the Bolsheviks consolidated their power prior to the outbreak of the Civil War. The Cheka was established soon after the Revolution. Lenin was worried that many would oppose his new government and used the Cheka to hunt down his political enemies. After an assassination attempt, Lenin launched the Red Terror which helped him to hold onto power by helping him to crush his enemies.

Develop the detail

Below are a sample exam-style question and a paragraph written in answer to this question. The paragraph contains a limited amount of detail. Annotate the paragraph to add additional detail to the answer.

> How far did Lenin rely on peace with Germany to secure his regime in the first six months?

> To a certain extent peace with Germany did help Lenin secure his regime. The war had become very unpopular with many Russians. Lenin sent one of his key supporters to negotiate a peace treaty. The terms of the treaty were very harsh but Lenin convinced fellow Bolsheviks to support the treaty. Peace with Germany clearly helped Lenin to secure power in the sense that it ended an unpopular war. However, it also created new problems because the peace treaty was also unpopular.

Section 4: Keeping and consolidating power, 1918–1924

The causes of the Russian Civil War

The beginning of the Civil War

The rebellion of the **Czech Legions** on 25 May 1918 signalled the start of the Civil War. During the summer of 1918, counter-revolutionary armies were established in Siberia, Estonia and in the Ukraine.

At the beginning of the Civil War, it was far from obvious that the **Reds** would win. The Red Army only occupied one-fifth of Russia. Lenin was even forced to make Moscow Russia's new capital, as White forces threatened Petrograd.

> ### Red, White and Green
> The Communists' opponents were known as the '**Whites**' and the Communist forces were referred to as the 'Reds'. Trotsky was appointed Head of the Red Army and Admiral Kolchak was declared Supreme Ruler of the Whites in November 1918. General Yudenich in Estonia and General Denikin in southern Russia recognised Kolchak's authority in the summer of 1919. Another group who opposed both the Reds and Whites were the '**Greens**', who supported economic power being transferred to local groups of peasants.

Causes

Many factors contributed to the outbreak of the Civil War:

- By July 1918 Russia had become a one-party state dominated by Lenin and the Communist Party. Other parties supported the Whites, and wished to remove the Communists from power.
- Others fought the Communists because they wanted a return to the Tsar's regime or the return of the Provisional Government.
- The British and French wanted Russia to remain in the war against Germany and did not want to see the emergence of a communist regime in Russia. The Japanese wanted to expand their territory and influence.
- Foreign countries such as Britain and France sent troops to Russia and provided the Whites with supplies, which allowed the Civil War to develop in 1918. The British landed troops at the port of Murmansk and the French occupied Odessa. Japan took control of Vladivostok.
- The Czech Legion in 1917 was created out of Austro-Hungarian prisoners, who now fought for the Allies in the hope of creating their own country once Austria–Hungary had been defeated. The Legion consisted of 40,000 men and opposed the Red Army.
- Many different nationalities within the pre-1914 Russian Empire, such as the Finns, Ukranians and Poles, wanted to create their own countries. They therefore fought against the Bolsheviks.
- Many Russians opposed the Treaty of Brest-Litovsk. The left-wing Socialist Revolutionaries abandoned their coalition with the Communists in March 1918, and opposed Lenin. They were involved in the assassination attempt on Lenin.
- The Bolsheviks started to clash with the peasantry. Lenin authorised the forcible collection of grain stocks from the peasants to feed the cities and the Red Army. This policy was popular in the towns and cities but not with the peasants. Peasants avoided conscription and took steps to hide their grain.
- Lenin increased the oppression of the peasants, but grain production continued to decline and some peasants supported the Greens and the Whites.

Mind map

Creating a mind map will help you answer the following question:

Why did Civil War begin in Russia in 1918?

Use the information on the opposite page to add detail to the mind map below. Remember to identify links and the most important cause on your mind map.

- The role of Communist policies
- The role of the Czech Legion
- The role of different nationalities
- The role of the Whites
- The role of foreign countries

The causes of the Civil War

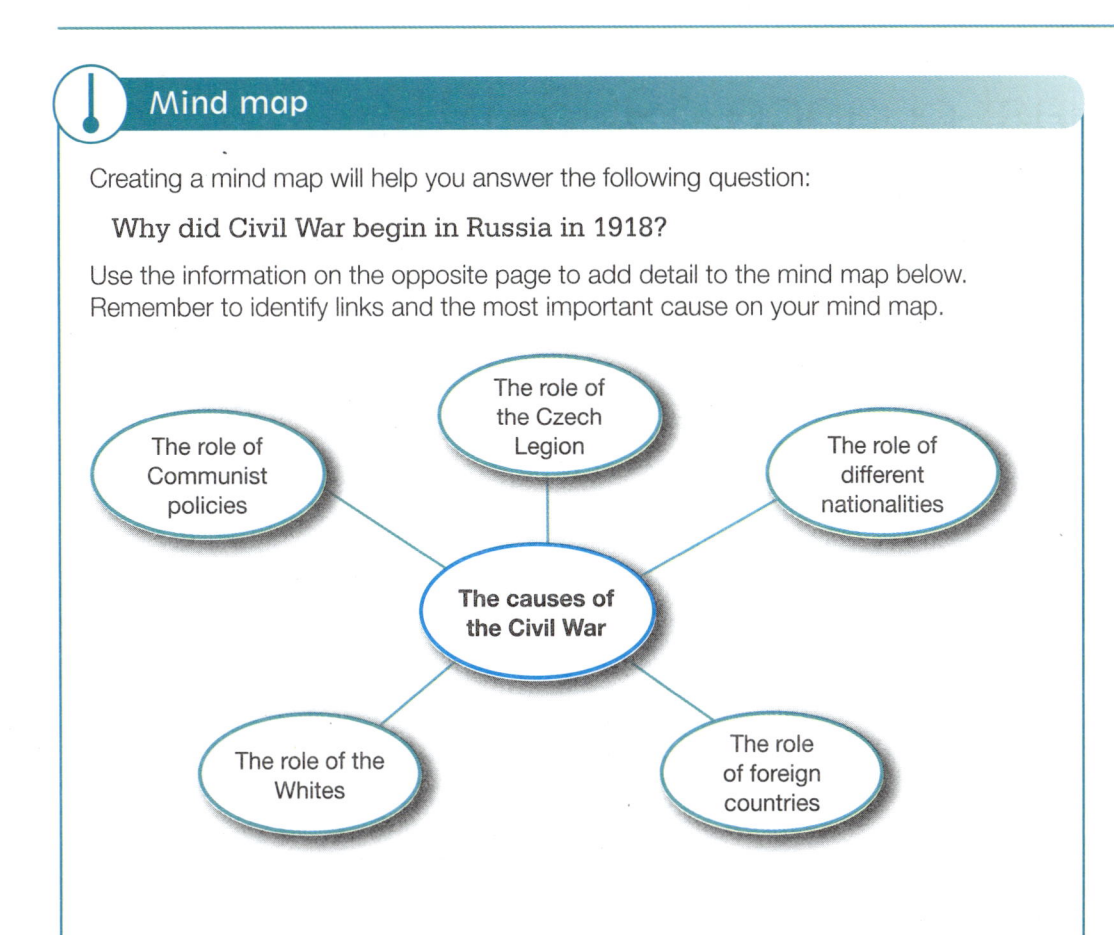

Complex essay style

Below are a sample exam-style question, a list of key points to be made in the essay, and a simple introduction and conclusion for the essay. Read the question, the plan, and the introduction and conclusion. Rewrite the introduction and the conclusion in order to develop an argument.

Why did Civil War begin in Russia in 1918?

Key points:
- The role of Communist policies.
- The role of the Whites.
- The role of foreign countries.
- The role of the Czech Legion.
- The role of different nationalities.

Introduction

There were different reasons why Civil War began in 1918. These were opposition to Communist policies and the role of the Whites, the intervention of foreign countries, the Czech Legion and the impact of different nationalities. All these factors contributed to the Civil War.

Conclusion

Overall there were different reasons why the Civil War began in 1918. These were opposition to Communist policies and the role of the Whites, the intervention of foreign countries and the Czech Legion and finally, the impact of different nationalities. Opposition to Communist policies was the most important reason for the Civil War.

Section 4: Keeping and consolidating power, 1918–1924

Reasons for the Communist victory and the importance of War Communism

Why did the Reds win the Civil War?
A range of factors contributed to the Communist victory during the Civil War:

White weaknesses
- They lacked a unified command structure and strategy.
- The Whites were spread out over large geographical areas.
- They often failed to co-ordinate attacks. For example, General Deniken's forces were concentrated in the south-east of Russia. He failed to co-ordinate his attacks with Kolchak effectively, and his forces were defeated.
- They lacked support from many Russians, who identified the Whites with former Tsarist supporters or foreign invaders.
- The Whites failed to work effectively with the Greens, led by Nestor Makhno. The Greens controlled a peasant army, and wanted to give more political and economic power to the peasants. The Reds defeated Makhno's forces in 1919.

Red military strengths
- Trotsky used officers who had fought for the Tsar, which provided the Reds with more experienced leaders.
- Trotsky's Red Army controlled important railway routes, making it easier to transport troops.
- The Red Army successfully defeated each White army and prevented them working together effectively. In 1920 only one White army remained. It was led by General Wrangel, and was located in the Crimea. The Communists also defeated his army in 1920.

War Communism
- War Communism describes economic policies the Communists introduced during the Civil War to help achieve victory.
- The Communists controlled the industrial centres.
- Industry was nationalised and factories were converted to produce military supplies and equipment.
- It also involved a policy of requisitioning food from the peasants by force to ensure the industrial workers and Red Army were supplied with food. These policies helped the Communists win the Civil War.
- War Communism allowed the Bolsheviks to maintain war supplies essential for the Red Army during the Civil War.

Red leadership
- They had a unified leadership under Lenin.
- Trotsky was a very effective leader of the Red Army. This could be seen when he sent reinforcements to Petrograd and prevented General Yudenich from seizing control of Petrograd.
- Trotsky enforced strict discipline and used political officers within the army to ensure loyalty.
- Trotsky used an armoured train to visit and support areas under threat.
- Lenin used the Cheka to eliminate political opposition.

Foreign intervention
- By the end of 1919 foreign forces from Britain, France and the USA had left Russia.
- Foreign forces stopped supporting the Whites after the armistice had been signed with Germany to end the First World War.
- Foreign leaders realised the Whites would not win the Civil War. This weakened the Whites even further. Admiral Kolchak originally had the support of 30,000 foreign troops. However, by July 1919 the Red Army had defeated Kolchak's forces.
- During 1919 Polish forces had invaded the Ukraine and captured Kiev. Lenin ordered an invasion of Poland and by 1920 the Red Army had advanced to the Polish capital of Warsaw, where it was defeated. In April 1921 the Treaty of Riga was signed between Russia and Poland.

Eliminate irrelevance

Below are a sample exam-style question and a paragraph written in answer to this question. Read the paragraph and identify parts of the paragraph that are not directly relevant to the question. Draw a line through the information that is irrelevant and justify your deletions in the margin.

How far was Lenin responsible for the Communist victory during the Civil War?

> Lenin performed a significant role in achieving victory during the Civil War because he supported the introduction of War Communism. This economic policy involved the nationalisation of key factories, which allowed the Communists to convert these factories to produce supplies and weapons for the Red Army. Lenin also took the decision to forcibly requisition grain from the peasants, which meant the Communists could keep the Red Army and cities supplied with food. This policy helped to ensure the victory of the Communists. Lenin was not afraid to take important decisions, such as introducing the NEP in 1921. He also increased Communist political power by closing the Constituent Assembly in January 1918, which prevented the Assembly from becoming a centre of opposition. Lenin also took the decision to support the Red Terror, which undermined opposition to the Communists and helped them win the Civil War. Many different nationalities existed in Russia and they all wanted independence. In this way, Lenin played a significant role in achieving victory during the Civil War because he adopted the political and economic policies necessary for success.

RAG – Rate the timeline

Below are sample exam-style questions and a timeline. Read the questions, study the timeline and, using three coloured pens, put a Red, Amber or Green star next to the events to show:

Red: Events and policies that have no relevance to the question.

Amber: Events and policies that have some significance to the question.

Green: Events and policies that are directly relevant to the question.

1. Why did the Communists win the Civil War?

Now repeat the activity with the following questions:

2. How far was Trotsky responsible for the Communist victory during the Civil War?

3. To what extent were the weaknesses of the Whites responsible for the Communist victory during the Civil War?

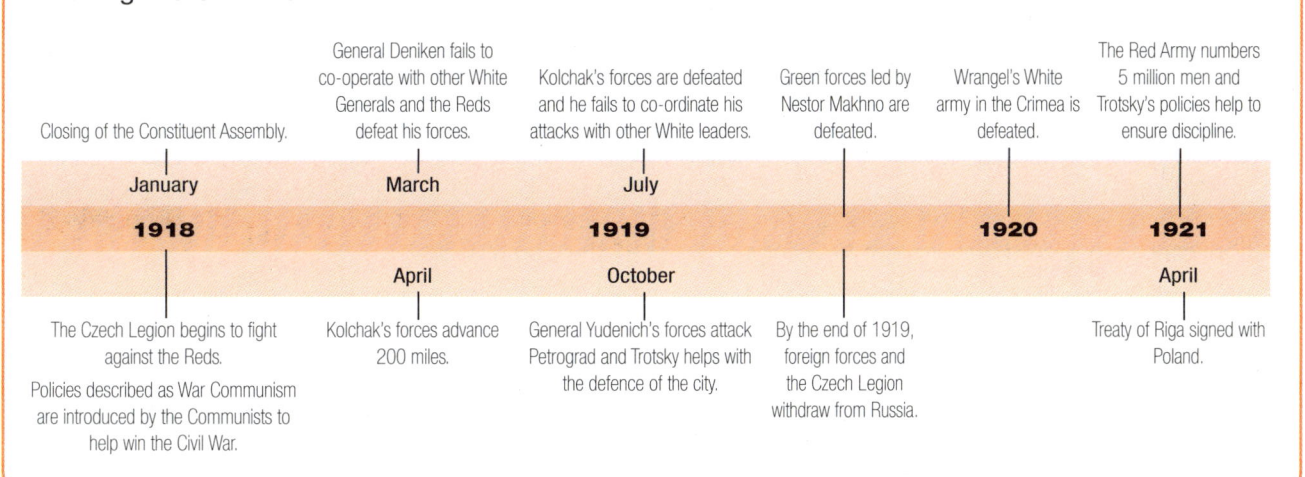

Timeline:

- **January 1918**: Closing of the Constituent Assembly.
- **April 1918**: The Czech Legion begins to fight against the Reds. Policies described as War Communism are introduced by the Communists to help win the Civil War.
- **March 1919**: General Deniken fails to co-operate with other White Generals and the Reds defeat his forces.
- **April 1919**: Kolchak's forces advance 200 miles.
- **July 1919**: Kolchak's forces are defeated and he fails to co-ordinate his attacks with other White leaders.
- **October 1919**: General Yudenich's forces attack Petrograd and Trotsky helps with the defence of the city.
- **1919**: Green forces led by Nestor Makhno are defeated. By the end of 1919, foreign forces and the Czech Legion withdraw from Russia.
- **1920**: Wrangel's White army in the Crimea is defeated.
- **1921**: The Red Army numbers 5 million men and Trotsky's policies help to ensure discipline.
- **April 1921**: Treaty of Riga signed with Poland.

Section 4: Keeping and consolidating power, 1918–1924

The causes and impact of New Economic Policy (NEP)

Problems facing Russia in 1921
Once victory had been achieved against the Whites in 1921, Lenin began to focus on rebuilding the Russian economy.

Famine
War Communism had resulted in peasants hoarding grain, which by 1921 had resulted in widespread famine and unrest throughout Russia.

Opposition from outside the party
Due to the famine, rebellions occurred against the Communists, such as the Tambov Uprising. The most serious rebellion was in March 1921, when the Kronstadt Rebellion took place. The Kronstadt Sailors had supported the Communists in the October Revolution. In 1921, many of the sailors were from peasant backgrounds and knew of the impact of War Communism, therefore they rebelled against Lenin and demanded:

- an end to the political domination of the Communists
- relaxation of War Communism and centralised economic control
- restoration of freedom of speech and press.

Opposition from within the party
Many communists viewed the NEP as a betrayal of **communism** because it allowed peasants to sell some of their produce for profit. It also permitted the owners of small factories to sell goods for profit.

Lenin's responses
Lenin used forceful **repression** and economic reform to secure his and the Communist Party's position in 1921:

The ban on factions
Lenin realised there was a danger that the Communist Party would be weakened by divisions. Therefore Lenin introduced a ban on **factions** within the Communist Party. Members of the Communist Party were not allowed to form groups that were independent from Lenin's control. Lenin also supported 'democratic centralism', which meant all other political parties were banned and decisions made by Lenin and the **Politburo** had to be supported by all Communists.

The impact of the NEP
In many ways, the NEP had a positive impact:

- Food shortages and the famine stopped by the end of 1921.
- In 1923, 85 per cent of companies were owned privately.
- Cultivated land and livestock increased.
- By 1926 the economy had almost returned to the production levels of 1913.

However, there were also negative results:

- Production of more crops resulted in falling agricultural prices and less income for peasants.
- The cost of industrial goods increased to a level that the peasants could not afford, because of their falling incomes.
- Some communists saw the NEP as leading Russia towards **capitalism** and away from the ideals of communism.

Repression	Economic reform
• Lenin ordered Trotsky to end the Kronstadt Rebellion by force. • Trotsky used 50,000 elite Red Army troops to attack the sailors. • It took three weeks to end the rebellion. • Thousands were killed or were sent to **Gulags**.	• At the Tenth Party Congress in March 1921, Lenin announced the end of War Communism. • He announced the introduction of the NEP. • Lenin hoped the NEP would strengthen the Russian economy, and that this would reduce opposition to the Communists. • Peasants could now privately sell part of their produce for profit but they would have to pay tax. • Private trading would be allowed, which resulted in the emergence of the '**Nepmen**'. • A new currency was introduced in 1922.

Spectrum of significance

Below are a sample exam-style question and a list of general points, which could be used to answer the question. Use your own knowledge and the information on the opposite page to reach a judgement about the importance of these general points to the question posed. Write numbers on the spectrum below to indicate their relative importance. Having done this, write a brief justification of your placement, explaining why some of these factors are more important than others. The resulting diagram could form the basis of an essay plan.

How far was the NEP successful?

1. Impact of the NEP on the famine.
2. Opposition from some communists to the NEP.
3. Secure Communist power.
4. Impact of the NEP on the economy.
5. Impact of the NEP on the peasants.

⟵───────────────────────────⟶

Very successful   Not very successful

Identify an argument

Below are a series of definitions, a sample exam-style question and two sample conclusions. One of the conclusions achieves a high level because it contains an argument. The other achieves a lower level because it contains only description and assertion. Identify which is which. The mark scheme on page 3 will help you.

Description: a detailed account.
Assertion: a statement of fact or an opinion that is not supported by a reason.
Reason: a statement that explains or justifies something.
Argument: an assertion justified with a reason.

How significant was the NEP in allowing Lenin to secure the Communist regime?

Sample 1

The NEP was very significant because it helped to reduce food shortages and end the famine which War Communism had caused. Allowing the peasants to sell their produce privately increased agricultural production and helped end the hoarding of grain by peasants, which had contributed to the famine of 1921. The NEP also stimulated economic recovery after the Civil War, which meant workers in the cities were less likely to rebel against the Communists. Moreover, the NEP was important because Lenin realised some Communists opposed the NEP and he used this as an excuse to strengthen his dictatorship by banning factionalism and ensuring all Communists followed Lenin's and the Politburo's decisions.

Sample 2

The NEP helped end food shortages and the famine which War Communism and forced grain requisitioning had caused. Peasants were allowed to sell their produce privately, which increased agricultural production and helped end the hoarding of grain by peasants, which had contributed to the famine of 1921. The NEP also stimulated economic recovery after the Civil War. Lenin also used the introduction of the NEP to strengthen the Communist dictatorship by banning factionalism and ensuring all Communists followed Lenin's and the Politburo's decisions. Therefore the NEP was very important.

Section 4: Keeping and consolidating power, 1918–1924

The establishment of the USSR in 1922 and the death of Lenin

Revised

Securing the regime

After 1921, Lenin took further steps to secure the Communist regime:

- After 1921, only the Communist Party could field candidates for election to the Soviets.
- All other political parties were banned.
- Increased use of propaganda that glorified the Communists and Lenin.
- Only Communist newspapers such as *Pravda* could be published.
- In 1922 the Cheka was replaced by the GPU, which remained a political police force.
- Gulags were expanded. In 1920 there were 84 camps and by 1923 there were 315.
- Show-trials of leading members of the clergy and Socialist Revolutionaries took place.
- Universities lost all their autonomy.

Establishment of the Union of Soviet Socialist Republics (USSR)

The USSR was established on 29 December 1922 and consisted of:

- the Russian Soviet Federative Socialist Republic (RSFSR)
- the Ukrainian Social Republic
- the Belorussian Soviet Socialist Republic (modern Belarus)
- the Transcaucasian Soviet Socialist Republic (Georgia, Armenia and Azerbaijan).

These areas had been part of the Russian Empire and by the end of 1921 the Communist Party had regained control of this territory. Many different nationalities lived in the USSR. Lenin believed the USSR could help overcome ethnic divisions, which may have threatened communism. Each republic within the USSR had their own government as part of a **federal** system. The individual republics sent representatives to a Congress of Republics and, combined with the Congress of Soviets, this formed the national **parliament** of the USSR. However, real political power was retained by the Politburo in this system. After 1922 Lenin had complete control over the Communist Party and government.

Lenin's death

In August 1918 a Socialist Revolutionary shot Lenin in the neck. Over the next two years Lenin recovered from this assassination attempt. However, in 1921 he began to suffer from side effects of the shooting and reduced his involvement in the government. On 25 May 1922 Lenin suffered a stroke from which he recovered. However, on 15 December 1922 he experienced a second stroke and then a third stroke shortly afterwards. Lenin then started to dictate his last **Testament**. In this document he made the following points regarding leading Communists:

- He acknowledged that Trotsky was talented but could be arrogant and failed to create effective working relationships with leading Communists.
- He criticised Kamenev and Zinoviev for not initially supporting the proposed take-over of power in October 1917.
- He stated that Stalin should be removed from the top branches of the Communist Party because he was 'too coarse'.

On 10 March 1923 Lenin suffered another massive stroke, which left his speech severely impaired. He was no longer an active member of the government, and died on 21 January 1924. Stalin, with the co-operation of Kamenev and Zinoviev, kept the content of Lenin's Testament secret.

You're the examiner

Below are a sample exam-style question and a paragraph written in answer to this question. Read the paragraph and the mark scheme provided on page 3. Decide which level you would award the paragraph. Write the level below, along with a justification for your decision.

How far had Lenin secured Communist power in the USSR by 1924?

> Lenin's political reforms following 1922 helped to secure Communist power to a significant extent. The establishment of the USSR in 1922 allowed the Communists to exert political control over former areas of the Russian Empire. Even though it adopted a federal structure, the Communist Party and the Politburo dominated the whole system. Only Communists could stand in elections to the Soviets and the leaders of the different republics had to be authorised by the Politburo. Additionally, during the period 1922–1924, the Gulags were expanded and the political police, now known as the GPU, continued to arrest and imprison political opponents. In this way, Lenin's political reforms following 1922 played an important role in securing Communist power because they tightened Communist control over the Russian regions and over political opponents.
>
> Level: _____
> Reason for choosing this level:
> _____
> _____

Turning assertion into argument

Below are a sample exam-style question and a series of assertions. Read the exam-style question and then add a justification to each of the assertions to turn it into an argument.

How far was Lenin successful in securing Communist control over the USSR by 1924?

> Lenin's creation of the USSR was very successful in securing control in the sense that
> _____
> _____
>
> Lenin's expansion of the Gulags helped secure Communist control in the sense that
> _____
>
> Lenin's refusal to allow freedom of speech and the press was successful in securing Communist control by 1924 in the sense that
> _____
> _____

Section 4: Keeping and consolidating power, 1918–1924

Exam focus

Revised

Below is a sample A grade essay. Read it and the examiner comments around it.

> How far do you agree that Lenin was the main reason for the consolidation of Communist control over Russia in the period from the outbreak of Civil War to Lenin's death in 1924?

The introduction reveals a clear understanding of the question and sets out a reasoned judgement.

Lenin was clearly the main reason for the consolidation of Communist control over Russia from the outbreak of civil war to Lenin's death in 1924. Lenin made key decisions during the period before the Civil War, during the Civil War and after the Civil War, whereas Trotsky was only important until 1921, and divisions in the opposition during the Civil War were of no importance before or after the Civil War. In this sense Lenin was continually working to keep the Communists in power and therefore the most important factor in their consolidation of power.

The candidate has included precise facts to support and develop their arguments, extending the range of the essay by discussing the Civil War.

During the Civil War, Lenin's most crucial decision was to support the introduction of War Communism. This economic policy allowed the Communists to take over factories and ensure production kept the Red Army supplied with weapons and equipment during the Civil War of 1918–1921. Moreover, this economic policy requisitioned grain from the peasants, ensuring that the cities and the Red Army continued to receive food supplies during the Civil War. Clearly, Lenin's support for War Communism played a crucial role in the Communist consolidation of power during the Civil War in the sense that it prioritised supplying the army over the immediate popularity of the regime.

The candidate links other factors such as the role of Trotsky but uses this factor to emphasise the importance of Lenin.

However, there were other important ways in which the Communists consolidated their power. Trotsky independently made some very important decisions during the Civil War. He supported the recruitment of ex-Tsarist officers, whose leadership during the Civil War helped to secure a Communist victory. It was Trotsky who effectively utilised the Russian railway network system to oppose threats by the Whites, such as General Yudenich's attack on Petrograd. Trotsky also played a key role in leading troops to crush the dangerous rebellion by the Kronstadt Sailors in 1921. Trotsky's role was also important because he took important tactical decisions which enabled the Bolsheviks to win the Civil War and consolidate their hold on the peace that followed.

The candidate shows a clear awareness of 'other factors' and analyses them effectively without contradicting previous arguments.

It could also be argued that weaknesses and divisions amongst the enemies of the Communists allowed the Communists to secure their regime. The Socialist Revolutionaries and Mensheviks failed to co-operate effectively to prevent the closing of the Constituent Assembly. Both parties were also divided amongst themselves, and some Socialist Revolutionaries briefly joined a coalition with the Communists. During the Civil War the Whites were geographically divided and failed to co-ordinate attacks on the Communists.

White leaders such as Admiral Kolchak and General Deniken did not co-operate effectively, and once foreign support was withdrawn from the Whites their position was weakened further. Clearly, the weaknesses of the Communists' opponents during the Civil War helped the Bolsheviks to consolidate their power because they never had to deal with the full force of a united opposition.

Lenin was undoubtedly the most important reason for the Communists' consolidation of power between the end of the Civil War and his death in 1924. In 1921, Lenin realised that War Communism had resulted in a famine and that this could lead to further opposition to the Communists, such as the Kronstadt Revolt. Therefore, Lenin decided to introduce New Economic Policy (NEP), which allowed small businessmen and peasants to sell goods for profit. This allowed the economy to recover from the chaos of the First World War and the Civil War, and reduced the risk of revolution against the Communists. Lenin also supported the establishment of the USSR in 1922, in an attempt to tie different nationalities more closely to the Communists and prevent ethnic divisions, which could threaten Communist power. Lenin's actions after the Civil War were extremely important because they created political stability across the whole of the country.

Lenin played the most important role in the consolidation of Communist power between the revolution and his death. During the Civil War, Lenin's support of War Communism and his appointment of Trotsky ensured a Communist victory and after the Civil War, Lenin made sure the Communists won the peace by introducing the NEP and creating the USSR. Certainly Trotsky played a role in the Civil War, as did divisions on the White side, but in the long term it was Lenin who worked tirelessly following the Revolution to guarantee the consolidation of Communist power.

The candidate once again analyses other factors, which are supported with precise facts. This allows the essay to have more balance and is not just focused on the 'given factor', which is the role of Lenin.

The candidate reaches a powerful conclusion emphasising the significance of Lenin over the whole period, but also shows an awareness of the significance of other factors.

30/30
This essay would gain high Level 5. The answer is well structured and considers a range of factors. Importantly, the answer takes the time frame specified in the question seriously, and analyses Lenin's role in three distinct periods. The final judgement reflects this sustained analysis and therefore the essay gets the top mark in Level 5.

What makes a good answer?

You have now considered four sample A grade essays. Use these essays to make a bullet-pointed list of the characteristics of an A grade essay. Use this list when planning and writing your own practice exam essays.

Timeline

1881

Assassination of Alexander II.

Alexander III becomes the new Tsar.

1892–1903

Sergei Witte serves as Minister of Finance and marks a period of rapid industrialisation known as the Great Spurt.

1894

Alexander III dies.

Nicholas II becomes the new Tsar.

1903

The Social Democratic Party splits into the Mensheviks and Bolsheviks.

1904–05

The Russo-Japanese War.

1905

Massacre of protesters in St Petersburg by troops loyal to the Tsar, known as Bloody Sunday.

Japanese forces defeat Russian troops and take control of Port Arthur.

Russian naval fleet is defeated at the Battle of Tsushima in May.

The height of the Russian Revolution.

The introduction of the October Manifesto.

1906

The Tsar issues the Fundamental Law, which becomes Russia's new constitution.

Establishment of the Duma.

Stolypin becomes Prime Minister.

1907

Second Duma is created in February, but is replaced by the Third Duma in November.

1911

Stolypin is assassinated.

1912

Fourth Duma replaces the Third Duma.

1912–13

Balkan Wars and rising tensions in Europe.

1914

Assassination of the heir to the Austro-Hungarian Empire, the final trigger cause for the First World War.

Russian forces defeated at the battle of Tannenberg.

1915

Tsar declares himself Commander-in-Chief.

1916

Murder of Rasputin by Prince Yusupov.

1917

Tsar abdicates.

Provisional Government led by Prince Lvov takes power.

A system of Dual Government emerges with the Petrograd Soviet.

1917

Lenin returns from exile to St Petersburg.

April Theses released.

1917

The Provisional Government launches an offensive against Austro-Hungarian forces, which fails and leads to widespread discontent across Russia known as the July Days.

Kerensky becomes leader of the Provisional Government.

General Kornilov marches on Petrograd.

Kerensky issues weapons to Bolsheviks to defend Petrograd.

Kornilov's forces fail to reach Petrograd.

Lenin and the Bolsheviks seize power and replace the Provisional Government.

1918

Lenin orders the closing of the Constituent Assembly.

Treaty of Brest-Litovsk.

The Tsar and his family are executed by the Communists.

1918–21

The Russian Civil War.

1920

The last White Army led by General Wrangel is defeated in the Crimea.

1921

Widespread famine and the Kronstadt Revolt.

Lenin replaces War Communism with the NEP.

Peace Treaty of Riga signed between Russia and Poland.

1922

The Union of Soviet Socialist Republics (USSR) is established.

The Cheka is replaced by the GPU (State Political Administration).

1922–23

Lenin suffers from repeated strokes and his active participation in government declines.

1924

Lenin dies and his written Testament is suppressed.

Glossary

Abdication When a monarch steps down from their position as king or queen.

Agrarian reforms Changes made by a government which are aimed at improving farming and harvesting within a particular country.

Autocracy Government that is dominated by an individual who has complete authority.

Bolsheviks The name of the political party led by Lenin, which took power in Russia in October 1917. They believed that a small group of professional communist revolutionaries would seize power in Russia instead of waiting for the masses to rise up in revolt.

Bolshevik Central Committee Represented the leading members of the Bolshevik Party, where key decisions were taken.

Bourgeoisie In modern terms the word is used to describe the middle classes. When Karl Marx originally used the term it described 'the owners of the means of production'.

Capitalism An economic system which encourages the private ownership of industry and the creation of profits for individuals.

Cheka Political police force established by Lenin to help the Communists secure their power in Russia.

Chief Procurator of the Holy Synod A powerful position within the Russian Orthodox Church.

Civil servants People who work for the government of a country.

Civil War This is when people from the same country fight each other in armed conflict.

Commissars People who are responsible for political education within a communist country. Often they are used to promote communism and ensure that people do not criticise communism.

Communism The belief that private ownership should be abolished, and all work and property should be shared by the community. In the twentieth century it became a political movement based upon the ideas and writings of Karl Marx.

Conservative In early twentieth-century Russia a conservative would have been a supporter of established customs and values and would have been opposed to change or dramatic political reform.

Constituent Assembly An elected body from which a new government would be formed.

Constitutional government A political system in which there are a set of fundamental rules limiting the power of government, in order to protect the rights of the population from excessive government power.

Cossacks Expert horsemen from Southern Russia who served as elite fighters for the Tsars.

Coup Using violence to gain political power.

Czech Legion During the First World War, Czechs had been conscripted to the Austro-Hungarian Army and thousands had been taken prisoner. The Provisional Government promised to free the Czechs to fight against Germany and Austria–Hungary. The agreement collapsed when Lenin signed the Treaty of Brest-Litovsk. The Czechs rebelled and fought against the Communists.

Decree A law made by someone in authority.

Desertion This is when soldiers refuse to fight and follow orders. Instead, they leave their units and often head home. Desertion in most armies is punishable by imprisonment or execution.

Divine right The belief that a monarch has been chosen directly by God to rule.

Duma The name given to the new Russian Parliament established in 1905.

Factions Smaller groups of people with different aims and ideas but who all support and belong to the larger group or political party.

Federalism A political structure in which power is divided between the federal government and individual state governments. In the USSR, the Communist Party and the Politburo dominated the whole structure.

Greens This group fought against the Reds and the Whites. They drew support from peasants and their policies focused on redistributing land to the peasants.

Gulags Camps where people were forced to work. Many of the political opponents of the Communists were sent to these camps.

Kadets A radical liberal group, which emerged from the 1905 Revolution. They demanded further constitutional reforms from the Tsar.

Kronstadt naval base This was a large naval base located outside Petrograd. In 1917, the sailors of Petrograd had turned against the Tsar and the Provisional Government. They also posed a threat to Lenin and the Communists in 1921.

Land Captains Established by Alexander III's government to extend the power of the Tsar across the Russian Empire.

Left-wing In early twentieth-century Russia someone described as 'left-wing' would have been a supporter of socialism and would have been more radical in his or her political ideas.

Lenin He supported the ideas of communism. He became the leader of the Bolsheviks after they split from the Social Democratic Party in 1903.

Liberals This group supported free elections and a parliament. The Tsar would become a constitutional monarch similar to the British King or Queen. Liberals were mostly supported by the professional middle classes, such as doctors and lawyers. The 1905 Russian Revolution saw the emergence of two main liberal groups; the Kadets, who demanded further political reforms after 1905, and the Octobrists, who accepted the Tsar's reforms after 1905.

Manifesto A document outlining political policies and aims.

Marxism A theory put forward by Karl Marx in the nineteenth century. He argued that capitalist society based on private ownership of property resulted in the exploitation of the working classes. He believed the workers would rise up in revolution and overthrow their rulers. They would then introduce a socialist society run by the workers. This society would eventually result in communism, where nobody would be exploited and there would be no powerful state. Instead, the state would 'wither away' and people would live in small communities.

Mensheviks They believed that the workers would eventually rise up in revolution against the Tsar. They did not support the Bolshevik idea of a small group of professional revolutionaries seizing power.

Military Revolutionary Committee Leadership of armed forces loyal to the Petrograd Soviet, which included the Red Guard.

Mir A commune where peasants worked the land collectively. The elders of the 'Mir' ran the commune. If land needed to be redistributed on the 'Mir' this would be done by the elders. If peasants wanted to leave the 'Mir' they would need the permission of the elders.

Mutiny Open rebellion against authority by sailors or soldiers against their officers.

Nationalisation The process of the government taking control of a company or a whole industry.

Nepmen Private traders who emerged after the introduction of the NEP in 1921.

Octobrists Name given to those Russian politicians who had supported the introduction of the October Manifesto after the 1905 Russian Revolution.

Okhrana Secret police who focused on seeking out political enemies of the Tsar within the Russian Empire.

Order No. 1 This was issued by the Petrograd Soviet. This order required all officers in the army to be elected by their own troops.

Orthodoxy Conforming to traditional religious standards, behaviour or attitudes.

Parliament A place where laws are passed for a country.

Pavel Miliukov In 1905 he became the leader of the Kadets, a Liberal political group. He also became the Foreign Minister within the Provisional Government in 1917. He opposed the autocratic power of the Tsar.

People's Will A political group that opposed the autocratic rule of the Tsars. They were prepared to use violence against the Tsarist system of government to achieve political change.

Petitions A written document signed by a large group of people, listing demands for action from a government or authority.

Plehve He was Minister of Interior under Tsar Nicholas II and responsible for internal security within Russia. He was assassinated in 1904.

Pogroms Organised violence, typically against Jews in parts of the Russia Empire in the nineteenth and twentieth centuries.

Politburo Consisted of approximately nine Communists who met every week to make key political and economic decisions. During the Civil War they became even more significant than the Sovnarkom.

Proletariat Term used by Karl Marx to describe the industrial working classes.

Provisional Government It was established as a temporary government, formed from members of the Duma. Elections would be held when a new constitution was established.

Pytor Struve A leading liberal who supported the ideas of improved civil rights and more equality within Russia. He also opposed the Tsar's autocratic rule and expressed his opposition through his political writings.

Radicalism The act of supporting drastic change to the political, social and economic system of a country.

Red Guards Numbered approximately 10,000 men and were the elite fighting force of the Bolsheviks.

Reds Name given to the Communists fighting during the Civil War.

Reform To improve something by introducing positive changes.

Repression Restricting freedoms to increase power and control.

Russification The process by which Russian culture and language was forced upon different ethnic groups across the Russian Empire.

Serfs Peasants contracted to landowners to act as farm workers. It was very difficult if not impossible to break free from the contract.

Slums Section of a city that is overpopulated and experiences severe poverty and low living standards.

Social Democratic Party Their key aim was to make Russia a socialist state. They were mostly supported by workers in the cities, such as Moscow. In 1903, the Social Democrats divided into the Mensheviks and Bolsheviks. The Mensheviks believed in working with the masses and trade unions to take power. The Bolsheviks believed a small group of professional revolutionaries who could organise the workers would seize power.

Socialist Revolutionaries The key aim of this group was to give all land to the peasants. They supported the use of violence to achieve their aims. This group was mostly supported by the peasants, who formed the majority of the population.

Soviet Councils established by workers to help with local government. One of the most powerful Soviets was the Petrograd Soviet.

Sovnarkom The most powerful body within the Bolshevik government.

Stavka Name given to the Command Centre of the Russian Army in the First World War.

Tariffs Taxes placed on foreign goods to make imported goods more expensive than goods produced at home. This would encourage people to buy domestic goods and encourage the growth of the economy. However, this can result in other countries placing tariffs on goods from your country.

Testament A document dictated by Lenin, meant for release after his death. It made recommendations regarding the future of communism and the USSR. He also made comments regarding the strengths and weaknesses of different leading Communists.

Trans-Siberian Railway The railway line operated from Moscow to Vladivostok on the Pacific Coast. It was approximately 9600 kilometres in length. It was built to help open up Siberia's economic resources. Additionally it would help Russia to protect their political and military interests in Asia.

Trotsky Trotsky supported the ideas of Karl Marx and he opposed the regime of Tsar Nicholas II and the Provisional Government. In 1917 he returned to Russia and joined with Lenin and the Bolsheviks. He performed a key role in organising the Bolsheviks in the October 1917 revolution. In the Civil War he led the Red Army to victory over the Whites.

Victor Chernov He was the leader of the Socialist Revolutionaries and supported some of the ideas of Karl Marx. Many Socialist Revolutionaries did not support his cooperation with the Provisional Government.

War Industries Committee An organisation established by businessmen to help increase the production of weapons and ammunition.

Whites Fought against the Reds and consisted of different groups, such as ex-supporters of the Tsar and Provisional Government. This group was also supported by foreign troops.

Zemgor This organisation emerged from the joining together of the Zemstva and town Dumas and focused on helping the casualties of the First World War. It was established in June 1915.

Zemstva Form of government established originally by Alexander II in 1864.

Answers

Section 1: The challenges to the Tsarist state, 1881–1906

Page 7, Complete the paragraph

Sergei Witte's policies were successful in modernising Russia's economy by 1903 to a considerable extent. Witte wanted Russia to become a world power through industrialisation. He obtained loans from France in order to build the Trans-Siberian Railway. The railway was designed to promote better links across Russia and to stimulate industry. He raised taxes from the peasants to help support industrialisation, and between 1892 and 1903 there was considerable urbanisation as people moved from the countryside to get jobs in the cities. **Therefore, Witte's policies were successful in modernising Russia to a considerable extent because he was able to raise money and spend it on important projects designed to modernise Russia.**

Page 9, Spot the mistake

Sample 1

The sample paragraph does not get into Level 4 because the candidate does not support and develop their points with precise facts. Instead of just referring to advisers they could have explained the importance of Sergei Witte's policies.

Sample 2

This sample paragraph is more detailed but the candidate does not use the points to directly answer the question.

Page 11, Develop the detail

There were many different political groups that opposed the Tsarist system of government and they were divided to a considerable extent. The Social Democrats were a single united party when they were established in 1898. However, **in 1903 the party split between two different groups, known as the Bolsheviks and Mensheviks,** and they had different beliefs and aims. **The Bolsheviks believed that an elite group of communists could seize power. The Mensheviks disagreed and believed that a mass revolution by the workers would result in the Communists coming to power in Russia.** The Socialist Revolutionaries also emerged as an opposition group and had support from many Russians. They were also prepared to use violence like some other groups to achieve their aims. The Liberals wanted political reforms **such as the right to vote and the establishment of a Parliament** but the Tsar refused to meet most of their demands. **The Tsar firmly believed in divine right and therefore did not think he had to share power.** Therefore to a great degree political parties were divided amongst themselves and with each other in the period 1881–1905.

Page 11, Turning assertion into argument

The Social Democratic Party became very divided in the sense that **the Bolsheviks argued that a small group of professional communist revolutionaries could seize power whilst the Mensheviks argued that only a mass revolution by the workers would result in the Communists taking power.**

The Socialist Revolutionaries and the Liberals had different aims and methods in the sense that **the Liberals used more peaceful methods to gain political reform whilst the Socialist Revolutionaries were prepared to use violence to achieve their political aims.**

Revolutionary ideas appealed to many Russians in the sense that **they proposed much needed reform which the workers and peasants supported.**

Page 13, Eliminate irrelevance

The Tsar's failure to share political power undoubtedly led to the unrest of 1905. Peasants and workers were becoming increasingly frustrated by the Tsar's failure to resolve poor agricultural policies, repeated famines and poor living standards within the cities. Because of the Tsar's failure to introduce political reform, many workers and peasants supported political opposition groups such as the Socialist Revolutionaries. ~~One of the Tsar's leading advisers Sergei Witte helped to modernise the Russian economy by 1905.~~ Nicholas II also failed to listen to the political demands of a growing Russian middle class, many of whom wanted Russia to become a parliamentary democracy, which to a degree made rebellion more likely. ~~After 1905 the Tsar allowed the establishment of a Russian parliament known as the Duma.~~ The Tsar's failure to share real political power before 1905 did contribute to the protests and rebellions in 1905 to a substantial degree because he failed to give the peasants or workers any form of real political power.

Page 15, Develop the detail

The Tsar was largely successful in dealing with the problems he faced in 1905. Different political groups **such as the Socialist Revolutionaries** were very hostile to the Tsar especially after humiliating defeats against the Japanese **such as the Battle of Tsushima**. However, he successfully divided these groups by promising political reforms. **The Tsar issued the October Manifesto, which promised the establishment of a Russian Parliament known as the Duma. This reduced opposition amongst the Liberals to the Tsar.** These different groups **such as the Kadets and Mensheviks** often failed to agree on their political aims, which made it easier for the Tsar to secure his regime by the end of 1905. Importantly the Tsar retained the support of the armed forces although there some mutinies in the navy. **In June 1905 sailors mutinied on the battleship *Potemkin*.** He also set up a new political party called the **'Union of Russian People'** and some of his supporters killed some Russians who supported reform. Many opponents to the Tsar were arrested and the army crushed various protests ruthlessly. In this way, the Tsar, was largely successful in addressing the problems he faced in 1905 because he crushed the revolution without conceding real reform.

Section 2: Tsarism's last chance, 1906–1917

Page 19, Develop the detail

The Dumas had some successes in the period 1906–1914. They did pass some reforms, **the second Duma, which lasted from February to June 1907 passed important land reform**, which helped some Russians. **Further land reforms were passed by the third Duma, which lasted from November 1907 to June 1912.** On occasions the Dumas did work with the Tsar's government effectively. **This can be seen with the introduction of health and accident insurance programmes.** However, the extent of success should not be over-emphasised. There were tensions between the Duma and Tsar especially between 1906 and 1907. Many people could not vote in the elections to the Dumas as the vote was restricted to certain groups **which only included the richest 30 per cent of the male population** after 1907 and this weakened opposition groups within the Duma. In this way the Dumas were moderately successful because although they did pass some reforms, they were unable to democratise Russia.

Page 21, Turning assertion into argument

Stolypin's policies did have some impact on Russian peasants and agriculture in the sense that **they allowed a quarter of Russian peasants to leave their communes and work on their own land.**

Stolypin's policies had less impact in Russian cities in the sense that **most of his policies focused on agricultural reform.**

Stolypin's policies did not increase the influence of the Dumas in the sense that **they ensured that real political power remained with the Tsar, as seen by the closing of the First Duma after only 73 days.**

The Tsar's position in Russia was strengthened by Stolypin's policies in the sense that **they gave power to the wealthy, who were less likely to support reform.**

Page 23, Complete the paragraph

To a certain degree it could be argued that the defeat of the Russian army was inevitable because it had many weaknesses. At the beginning of the First World War, even though the Russian army gained initial advances, they were soon defeated at the Battles of Tannenberg and Masurian Lakes. These defeats revealed the poor organisation and leadership of the Russian army, which supports the argument that defeat was inevitable. This is further supported by the fact that in 1915 Russian artillery was restricted to three shells per day due to economic difficulties. The Russian army also had to retreat from Russian Poland in 1915. However, in 1916 General Brusilov launched a successful attack against the Austro-Hungarians. Despite this success it could still be argued that the defeat of the Russian army was inevitable because the Russian economy could not support a long war.

Page 25, Identify an argument

Sample 1 contains the argument.

Page 29, Eliminate irrelevance

The revolution did little to resolve the problems facing Russia. It resulted in the removal of the Tsar from power when he abdicated on 2 March 1917. The workers had carried out successful strikes throughout January 1917 and the establishment of the Petrograd Soviet in February gave them increased political influence. ~~The Tsar made himself Commander-in-Chief in 1915 and left the unpopular Tsarina with more political influence in Petrograd~~. However, the extent to which the revolution removed all difficulties Russia faced was limited in some ways because the new Provisional Government still had to contend with the war with Germany in March 1917. The revolution had not resulted in peace. The Provisional Government continued with the war against Germany ~~until being removed from power in October 1917 by the Bolsheviks~~ and the problems of food shortages and lack of equipment for the Russian army were not immediately resolved. Clearly, the Provisional Government only had a limited success in resolving the problems facing Russia because they never solved the key issues of peace, land and bread.

Page 29, Develop the detail

Describing the revolutionary events of 1917 as well planned would be inaccurate because the strikes in Russian cities were not immediately intended to bring down the Tsar. These strikes were often in response to food shortages. The streets of Petrograd saw large numbers of demonstrators in the period January to March 1917. **On 9 January 140,000 workers went on strike in Petrograd and 100,000 workers went on strike on 14 February.** In February some army units **such as the Cossacks** refused to fire on demonstrators and this was not part of a planned revolution. **On 26 February the elite Pavlovsky Life Guards refused to fire on demonstrators.** The Tsar failed to return to Petrograd and was convinced by close colleagues to abdicate. Therefore the extent of planning for the revolution was limited because the Duma and the army were reacting to events as they developed in the period January to March 1917.

Section 3: February to October 1917

Page 35, Complete the paragraph

Lenin's return to Russia weakened the Provisional Government to a significant extent because he provided the Bolsheviks with clear leadership, which posed a threat to the government. His April Theses emphasised the promise of 'Peace, Land and Bread'. He realised that many Russians opposed the continuation of the war against Germany and the decision by the Provisional Government not to seek peace. He also knew that many people viewed the Provisional Government as being dominated by landowners and the middle classes. Lenin also promised 'All Power to the Soviets,' which was a popular message. However, he did not attract the mass support of the Russian people in April 1917 and there were other important factors which weakened and threatened the Provisional Government. **Lenin weakened and threatened the government to a considerable degree because he provided clear leadership, which eventually resulted in the downfall of the Provisional Government in October 1917.**

Page 35, Turning assertion into argument

Lenin's return to Russia to a certain extent threatened the government in the sense that **he provided the Bolsheviks with clear leadership and direction.**

Lenin's promise of 'Peace, Land and Bread' was important in weakening the government to a certain degree in the sense that **it helped the Bolsheviks gain more support amongst the workers in key cities such as Petrograd.**

The significance of Lenin's return to Russia in April 1917 should not be over-emphasised and other factors to a considerable degree threatened the government in the sense that **the war continued to act as a source of discontent within Russia.**

Page 37, Develop the detail

General Kornilov's coup weakened the Provisional Government to a large extent. His decision helped Lenin and the Bolsheviks **because Kerensky, the leader of the Provisional Government, released Bolsheviks from prisons in Petrograd and provided them with weapons to oppose Kornilov.** The Provisional Government's Prime Minister, Kerensky, did not make wise choices when he discovered that Kornilov was marching on Petrograd **because now the Red Guards had weapons, which could be used to overthrow the Provisional Government.** Furthermore, the coup affected the popularity of the government and the Bolsheviks. **After the coup, the Bolsheviks won a majority of support in the Petrograd Soviet.** In this way, Kornilov's coup was an extremely important factor in explaining the failure of the Provisional Government because it both weakened the government and helped the opposition.

Page 39, Spot the mistake

The answer contains relevant points but the candidate has not linked these points explicitly to the question, which prevents the answer from accessing Level 4.

Page 41, Identify an argument

Sample 1 contains the argument.

Page 41, Spot the mistake

Here the candidate makes two mistakes. Firstly, the answer focuses on why the Bolsheviks attracted widespread support rather than the extent to which they attracted widespread support. Secondly, the supporting information is generalised. Therefore the answer gets a mark in Level 3 and cannot access Level 4.

Page 43, Eliminate irrelevance

The Bolsheviks were successful in taking power because other parties failed to exploit the weakness of the Provisional Government in October 1917. ~~The Tsar had always been unpopular and so had his German wife Alexandra. The Provisional Government was also unpopular especially after the failure of the June Offensive.~~ After the July Days the Mensheviks and Socialist Revolutionaries were closely associated with the Provisional Government and this weakened their support whilst support for the Bolsheviks increased, especially within the cities. This partially explains why the Bolsheviks were successful. Additionally, Lenin managed to convince the Bolshevik Central Committee to support an armed take-over of power whilst other political parties such as the Socialist Revolutionaries were not so decisive. ~~After gaining power, Lenin began to secure his regime and launched the Red Terror, supported by the Cheka, to support his political power.~~ Therefore, the Bolsheviks were successful in gaining power in October because Lenin successfully exploited the weaknesses of the Provisional Government.

Section 4: Keeping and consolidating power, 1918–1924

Page 49, Spot the mistake

The answer does not get into Level 4 because the answer lacks specific detail.

Page 49, Develop the detail

To a certain extent peace with Germany did help Lenin secure his regime. The war had become very unpopular with many Russians. **Indeed, it had led to the collapse of Kerensky's Provisional Government in October 1917.** Lenin sent **Trotsky**, one of his key supporters, to negotiate a peace treaty. **The treaty was signed in March 1918 and was called the Treaty of Brest-Litovsk.** The terms of the treaty were very harsh. **The Germans demanded a large slice of Russian territory including Latvia, Lithuania and Estonia. However,** Lenin convinced fellow Bolsheviks to support the treaty. Peace with Germany clearly helped Lenin to secure power in the sense that it ended an unpopular war. However, it also created new problems because the peace treaty was also unpopular.

Page 53, Eliminate irrelevance

Lenin performed a significant role in achieving victory during the Civil War because he supported the introduction of War Communism. This economic policy involved the nationalisation of key factories, which allowed the Communists to convert these factories to produce supplies and weapons for the Red Army. Lenin also took the decision to forcibly requisition grain from the peasants, which meant the Communists could keep the Red Army and cities supplied with food. This policy helped to ensure the victory of the Communists. ~~Lenin was not afraid to take important decisions such as introducing the NEP in 1921.~~ He also increased Communist political power by closing the Constituent Assembly in January 1918, which prevented the Assembly from becoming a centre of opposition. Lenin also took the decision to support the Red Terror, which undermined opposition to the Communists and helped them win the Civil War. ~~Many different nationalities existed in Russia and they all wanted independence.~~ In this way, Lenin played a significant role in achieving victory during the Civil War because he adopted the political and economic policies necessary for success.

Page 55, Identify an argument

Sample 1 contains the argument.

Page 57, You're the examiner

This answer would be awarded Level 4. The answer is focused and detailed, and clearly analyses why Lenin's measures helped to consolidate his power.

Page 57, Turning assertion into argument

Lenin's creation of the USSR was very successful in securing control in the sense that **he allowed no other political parties to exist in the USSR after 1921.**

Lenin's expansion of the Gulags helped secure Communist control in the sense that **thousands of political opponents had been arrested by the GPU and sent to the camps.**

Lenin's refusal to allow freedom of speech and the press was successful in securing Communist control by 1924 in the sense that **no opposition was tolerated from inside or outside the party and the doctrine of democratic centralism ensured all members of the party followed Lenin and the Politburo.**